Dr Bob Mayo is a fou ... the
Centre for Youth Min ... M),
currently the largest del ... ity
work training (Christia ... a
theologian, an ordained ... u-
cationalist and a practisin ... worker. He is
the author of *Gospel Exp*...

Dr Sara Savage has been lecturing in psychology, sociology and
research methods in the Cambridge Theological Federation for
the past seven years. Recent publications include *Psychology for
Christian Ministry* (with Fraser Watts and Rebecca Nye, Routledge, 2002), and a chapter in *Previous Convictions*, ed. Martin
Percy.

Dr Sylvie Collins is Senior Lecturer in the Sociology of Religion
at Kingston University and a contributor to *Calling Time*, ed.
Martin Percy (Sheffield Academic Press, 2000). Her research
interest and specialty is faith among young people.

Also by the authors and published by SPCK/Triangle

Bob Mayo, *Gospel Exploded: Reaching the Unreached* (Triangle, 1996).

Sara Savage, 'A Psychology of Conversion – from All Angles', in *Previous Convictions: Conversion in the Present Day*, ed. Martin Percy (SPCK, 2000).

Ambiguous Evangelism

Bob Mayo
with Sara Savage and Sylvie Collins

First published in Great Britain in 2004 by
Society for Promoting Christian Knowledge
36 Causton Street
London SW1P 4AU

British Library Cataloguing-in-Publication Data
A catalogue record for this book is available from the British Library

ISBN 0–281–05637–4

1 3 5 7 9 10 8 6 4 2

Typeset by Avocet Typeset, Chilton, Aylesbury, Bucks
Printed in Great Britain by Bookmarque Ltd, Croydon, Surrey

Acknowledgements

Thanks and appreciation are due to the Revd Professor Jeremy Begbie and the work of Theology through the Arts. The Rt Revd Graham Cray, Jane Hildreth and Liz Gulliford all contributed significantly to the youth and world view research project. Kathy Wilson, Jane Chevous, Tracey Bennett, Joy Martin, Steve Griffiths, Chris Rose and Chris Cocksworth are valued and valuable colleagues. Above all, though, thanks are due to Andy Lloyd for his wit, wisdom and insight.

Contents

———◦◦◦———

Introduction

There are two separate encounters that illustrate for me a shift in people's perception of Christianity. The first encounter was the deference shown to me, as an Anglican priest, from people of one generation. I was talking with two sisters about the funeral arrangements for their brother. 'There is no need for you to call me "Father",' I said to them. 'Please do call me "Bob".' 'All right, Father, whatever you want,' they replied. The second encounter was the confusion shown towards me by two people of a completely different generation. They asked me what I wanted to do with my life and I told them that I was a priest. They asked me why I had become a priest. I replied, 'Because it is the most honourable, privileged, worthwhile job that I could imagine; not only will I be listening to people and trying to help them but also I will be able to learn about and talk about God. I can't think of a better job to do.' There was a moment's pause before one of them, slightly bemused, replied, 'I think I am going to be a footballer.'

In my early years as an Anglican clergyman, I often found myself met with embarrassment because people did not know what they should say to me as a priest. Someone I played rugby with at the time remarked, 'Going out drinking with a priest is like going to the pub with my mother-in-law!' There was a period when I would shy away from getting involved in any conversation about religion. Generally, if someone said to me that they wanted to talk with me about Christianity, what they actually meant was that they wanted to tell me what they thought about it. It seemed that every time that I went to a party I would end up standing in the corner listening to someone tell me the reason why they did not like the Church. On one occasion, one person spent a whole hour telling me how, when he had gone for confession aged 13, he had seen the priest reading a newspaper, and that had disillusioned him. Having been brought up with such a clearly defined set of expectations about Christianity and the Church, he had a clear sense of what a priest should or should not be doing – and taking five minutes to read the paper between confessions did not fit his view of a priest. Now, as a 27-year-old man, he was still living out the reactions he had felt as a 13-year-old boy. My contention is that people, now, have less clear expectations of the Church because they have less knowledge of it.

Over the last few years, however, I have observed something of a sea change in the social climate: Christianity, as a topic of conversation, is increasingly met with polite interest rather than embarrassment. Nowadays, when I reveal that I am an Anglican priest, I am generally received with equanimity – and occasionally even enthusiasm. Nowhere is this more apparent than in younger generations: nine-year-old Oscar, for example, proudly presents me as his friend, 'Bob the vicar!' (always spoken to chime with *Bob the Builder*).

I also find it harder and harder to get anyone to disagree with me. However, this lack of disagreement is not an indication of agreement. People tell me that they find what I am saying interesting. They respect me for my convictions. They tell me that they are glad that I have got a faith, but it is not for them. It is not that people have rejected Christianity, but rather that they have never encountered it. People admire me for my faith as if I am a novelty, a rare species of being; they want me close enough to be interesting but not so close as to be threatening. There is often a kind of unspoken respect for the fact that I actually believe in something (anything!). 'You must understand', a high-powered executive said to me, 'people like me rarely get the chance to meet and talk with people like you.'

Introduction

'I find people endlessly interested but rarely challenged by the figure of Christ.' This sentiment was expressed by the minister of a Scottish church I attended while visiting friends in Edinburgh. Over the previous two days the minister had conducted a wedding and a funeral, and he described how at both he had had difficulty in getting people to disagree with what he said. People were always polite and interested enough to hear his point of view, but they would rarely engage enough even to contest what he was saying and so the conversation would not develop. It was an uninformed type of interest, revealing neither understanding nor any desire to explore the issue further.

This apparent decline in genuine engagement relates to a decline of general knowledge about the narrative of the Christian faith in contemporary UK society. As Cardinal Cormac Murphy-O'Connor, Archbishop of Westminster, admitted in September 2001, in Britain, Christianity as a backdrop to people's lives and moral decisions has now almost been vanquished. A report published by the Church of England's Mission and Public Affairs Council (2004) concluded that many in Britain now have minimal knowledge of the Christian faith; the Christian story is no longer at the heart of the nation.

This certainly rings true at the level of my own experience. I have lost count of how often I have been asked, for example, whether Aladdin was in the Bible. A lack of biblical knowledge was illustrated in a story recently told to me by a friend about a conversation overheard during the interval at a performance of *Jesus Christ Superstar*: when a lady commented that the second half was going to be really sad, her friend's response was, 'How do you know, have you seen the show already?'

When I attended a confirmation recently at Ely Cathedral, the bishop was greeted with a whisper from a ten-year-old in the pews, asking who he was. When his parents replied that he was a 'bishop', the child asked whether he moved diagonally. It was intended as a funny comment, but still, it was the rules of chess that provided the only framework the ten-year-old had in his head for interpreting the idea of a bishop.

The reality of a declining reserve of Christian knowledge in the public sphere is illustrated in many areas. These are just a few examples:

- In the Argos catalogue, an earring in the shape of a diamond cross is listed with an earring in the shape of a diamond dollar, an earring in the shape of a skull and crossbones and one in the shape of an England pennant.
- Pollsters Mori interviewed 1,001 people for the fifth anniversary of BBC1's *Heaven and Earth* show. Asked to identify pictures of various public figures, only 18 per cent correctly named Dr Rowan Williams as the Archbishop of Canterbury while 28 per cent recognized *Big Brother 4* (2003) winner, Cameron Stout. Half of the population could not name any of the four Gospels (Matthew, Mark, Luke and John) (*Sun*, 8 September 2003).
- Contestants vying for the opportunity to compete on the TV show *Who Wants to be a Millionaire?* all failed when asked to put the petitions of the Lord's Prayer into the correct order.
- 37 per cent of people in the UK said David Beckham was more influential in their lives than God (BBC poll, 'What the world thinks of God', shown on BBC2, 26 February 2004).
- Schools are being encouraged to introduce a six-term year. This is partly because the cost of holiday accommodation and travel rises dramatically during school holidays, so some families are taking holidays during term-time. A six-term year would prevent this happening. It is also partly because young children, especially, lose ground over the long summer holidays; shorter terms and shorter breaks would put less strain on both children and teachers (*Observer*, 15 February 2004). This would mean that school holidays would no longer automatically coincide with Easter.
- It was reckoned that there was a 'jinx' on teams using the southern changing room at the Millennium Stadium in Cardiff. A variety of approaches was tried, ranging from exorcism to a feng shui blessing that involved ringing a bell,

carrying incense sticks, throwing sea salt and leading a horse around the pitch to counter the bad spirits. Negative energy from the nearby media room was thought to be at the heart of the problem. The southern dressing room now has a picture of a horse and a phoenix on the wall, and this is seen as an effective antidote.

Observance of the Sabbath day is another marker that indicates shifting attitudes towards religion within UK society. When John Macey, an aspiring young footballer, was spotted playing in a game one Sunday in 1939, he received a letter from the FA, banning him from playing for his local club, Winchester City. The FA finally relented 50 years later and wrote again, telling him he was free to play once more; by then he was over 70 years old. Similarly, when the Wimbledon Lawn Tennis Association changed the Men's Finals from the Saturday to the Sunday, there was a storm of protest and the local church wrote to complain because it was seen as an infringement of the Sabbath. In 1994 legislation allowing Sunday trading was introduced in England. Now the idea of Sunday as a day for shopping and sporting occasions is accepted without question.

This shift in social consciousness is not exclusive to Britain; nevertheless it is noticeable that, in other countries, the religious framework remains a prevailing influence. Northern Ireland's shift in cultural habits, for example, lags behind the rest of the United Kingdom. There, the liberalization of betting laws in 2004 saw Ulster's first ever race meeting on a Sunday held at the Down Patrick Race Club. Protesting outside the Race Club, the Revd Trevor Baxter, minister of the Free Presbyterian Church at Ballyhaninch described the 'Sabbath desecrators' as 'lost souls' (*Independent*, 22 March 2004).

This book explores the circumstances of how the reservoirs of Christian knowledge within the UK have sunk so low that what is often described as a post-Christian society would be better described as a pre-Christian society. It is not that people have turned away from the Christian faith as the fact that they don't know anything about it. There is such a cursory understanding of Christianity that people are consequently neither curious nor hostile about the faith.

Ten years ago when I first recognized the reality of how little people knew of Christianity, I coined the phrase 'pre-non-Christian':

> In my perception there are three divides. There are Christians. There are 'non-Christians' and there are 'pre-non-Christians'. 'Non-Christians' are people who have had some contact with church or Christians and have some understanding of the framework of Christianity. The reason they are not Christians is either hostility, apathy or disagreement.
>
> 'Pre-non-Christians' are people who have little or no knowledge or understanding of Christ or Christianity. Jesus might be a word to be used negatively – nothing more than a swear word. The reason they are not Christians is not hostility, apathy or disagreement but ignorance of the basic Christian stories.
>
> Traditionally the Church has worked with 'non-Christians'. Until recently most of the country have been non-Christians and the reality of pre-non-Christians is not yet catered for in the Church's thinking. (Mayo, 1996:12–13)

This lack of exposure means that often people have not found out enough about Christianity to be either put off or drawn towards it. No one is going to be curious about the pink elephant in the next-door town if they don't know that there is a pink elephant to be curious about.

Ten years on from my 1996 work, this book draws on the conclusions of a two-year research project (Savage, Mayo and Collins [2005]) that looked at the world view of young people in Britain, as expressed through popular art and culture. The findings of the report pointed to an overwhelming lack of any knowledge about the Christian faith. We had hoped to have been able to draw out conclusions for the Church from the findings.

It was tempting to conclude that the issue was one of packaging, and that if Christianity was presented differently in an appropriate, user-friendly, accessible manner, then people would connect with the message. There is an increasing recognition from churches that they need to make Christianity authentic and relevant to young people; and many are restructuring their Sunday services, introducing midweek or youth services, and exploring the use of different media to give a more imaginative presentation of the Christian message.

The assumption here, however, is that the content of the message will be understood if it can be got across in an appealing way. Our conclusions from the research findings, however, were that this is not the case; the lack of an underpinning religious narrative means that people are not going to recognize the Christian message for what it is – however well it is presented.

Everyone has an underpinning narrative that shapes how they interpret something – hence the joke, 'I am not paranoid; it is just that everyone is out to get me.' My understanding of sexuality will be shaped according to how I see sexuality fitting into the context of people's relationship with each other and with God. My understanding of punctuation (e.g. what I think a full stop or a comma or a colon is intended to mean) will be defined by my understanding of language. My understanding of mathematics is going to be dictated by my understanding of numbers and what I want to use them for. This is essentially the thinking of the Jewish Hungarian scientist-turned-philosopher, Michael Polanyi (1891–1976). Polanyi considered that for something to be understood it needed to be appreciated in context. This was done by including a concept of purpose in the study of phenomena. Polanyi argued that any attempt rigorously to eliminate a concept of purpose from a picture of the world must lead to absurdity (Polanyi, 1983:3). Both living beings and machines have aims, functions and purposes or standards of rightness in which they can succeed or fail. A complete knowledge of the physical laws of a clock along with a detailed breakdown of the component parts and an exact prediction of all future configurations will not explain it as a clock. This can only be done with a knowledge of its function and purpose, namely to tell the time; 'This clock has not lost ten seconds in five years, therefore it is a good clock' (Polanyi, 1983:330). By the same logic, to have a real understanding of Christ as God and Saviour there needs to be some understanding of transcendence and spirituality beyond a mere existentialism.

In terms of evangelism, it is therefore a content issue as well as a process issue. For a lot of people there has to be a stage before the *Alpha* style of user-friendly gospel exploration, in which they are led from an ignorance about to an awareness of the Christian faith. In management learning terms, this stage is described as the transition from 'unconscious ignorance' to 'conscious ignorance' – it is the movement from not knowing what you don't know to knowing what you don't know. If people have never been aware of the Christian story, they are not going to feel the lack of it. People don't miss what they have never known. Once people are aware of the Christian story, then their interest can be aroused and they can go along to church on Sunday or access the variety of user-friendly methods of presenting the gospel that are on offer. This transition from ignorance to awareness is the territory of this book.

Initial conversations about the faith may occur in a snatched moment of conversation in a pub or school common room, in a chance encounter round a photocopier at work or while hanging out with friends. But it can no longer be assumed that these conversations will take place within a shared territory of understanding, nor that the actions of a company or of an individual are necessarily illustrative of an underpinning attitude towards God. If, for example, Victoria Beckham compares her husband to Jesus on the basis that they have similar hairstyles, she is not consciously trivializing the Son of God; she is simply making a comment on her husband's hairstyle. On the same level, a group of young people of my acquaintance wear rosaries as an indication of affiliation to their group and not as an indication of a commitment to or reaction against Catholicism. In a wider context, when my local Marks and Spencer store replaced, overnight

Stories / open-ended
engagement.

on 14 February, Valentine chocolates with Easter eggs, it was not a liturgical decision based on a Lenten preparation for Easter but simply a commercial decision as to what would sell.

So the question addressed in *Ambiguous Evangelism* is: how is it possible to share the message of Christianity in this context in a way that will get over the barrier of ignorance and enable people to interpret what they are hearing? If people know nothing and are told nothing about the Christian faith, then they will not be able to make an informed response to the claims of Christ. Even the film *The Passion of the Christ* might appear to be nothing more than a story about a man being crucified if none of the wider context is known.

This situation, though, is not answered by automatically giving out more information to people who might not know what you are talking about. If people who know nothing are told too much, too quickly, about the Christian faith, they can feel put off and judged. But information given at an appropriate level in a meaningful way can serve to encourage engagement. My contention is that faith has to be shared in a deliberately open-ended manner in order to elicit a response. Faith can be presented in such a way that people are encouraged to interpret what they are hearing; it is a style of evangelism that creates opportunities for people to form their own conclusions. Drane (2000) makes the point that telling the stories of the faith, relating them to our own personal stories, and discovering new images of Christ that will speak with power to today's generation may lead to a more open-ended sharing of the faith than some Christians would be happy with. But the very fact that stories leave spaces for meanings and create new opportunities for the exploration of spirituality means they will more effectively address the concerns of everyday life, cross cultural boundaries, and invite active interaction and participation from those who share in their telling.

God loves and reaches out to every individual person in God's unique and different ways. The son is the only way to the father, but there are many ways to Jesus Christ. (Fung, 2002:3)

The term I have coined for this approach to faith-sharing is 'ambiguous evangelism'. 'Ambiguous' and 'evangelism' may at first glance appear to be strange bedfellows. Ambiguity derives from a combination of two Latin words: *ambi* (in two ways) plus *agere* (lead, drive, act); hence the meaning: 'to lead two ways'. Evangelism, on the other hand, is about presenting the claims of one way: to evangelize, according to the Archbishop's statement of 1918, is 'to present Jesus in the power of the Holy Spirit, that men and women shall come to put their trust in God through him, to accept him as their Saviour and serve him as their King in the fellowship of his Church'.

Moreover, unease at ambiguity is ingrained. People like to know where they stand. It makes them feel safe. In a black-and-white world I can live knowing what's what. Acknowledging the existence of grey puts me in a position where every instance, choice and concept might need to be weighed up and could be open to debate. Such is the extra energy required to live with a world view where constant analysis is needed to deal with life that it becomes unattractive. But while ambiguity can produce discomfort, it also puts people in the position of having to engage in order to make sense. In presenting the faith, ambiguity can make a space that invites people to participate in the process of learning the story and then working through the implications of the life, death and resurrection of Jesus Christ.

If the idea of allowing ambiguity into the process of evangelism seems strange – even, perhaps, sacrilegious – then it might help to remember two things. The first is that in any portrayal of spiritual ideas, there is always a point where words become inadequate. In talking about God there will always be a gap between the words being used and the reality of God that they attempt to portray. Words themselves are only the symbols that we use to describe something that is, ultimately, indescribable. A deliberate use of ambiguity in conversation can draw people into that gap so that they can interact with and reflect on the reality of God for themselves. The second thing to remember is that a creative use of ambiguity can make people aware that there are things about Christianity that they do not understand. If ignorance is static, then conscious ignorance is creative because it can stimulate in people a desire to find out more.

The first three chapters of the book are scene-setting. This begins in Chapter 1 with Sylvie Collins providing an in-depth look at the wider evidence for a decline in people's understanding of Christianity. Chapter 2 looks at our youth and world view research project mentioned above, which examined young people's world view understood through popular art and culture. This is followed by a chapter that considers the nature of language and suggests that language is ultimately inadequate for talking about God – even if I might want to do so – and that all language is heard as an expression of choice or preference. This means that even if I say 'Jesus Christ rose from the dead', and mean it as fact, it is still heard as personal opinion.

This is followed by three 'what to do about it' chapters. Chapter 4 translates the principles of using parables into a modern context; Chapter 5 explains the principles of ambiguous evangelism, looking at the use of irony, play, challenge and dialogue; and Chapter 6 focuses on approaches to conducting conversations about Christ.

The final two chapters root the discussion within an understanding of identity and personhood. Ambiguity is inevitable when people do not understand what I might be talking about (see Chapter 3). Ambiguity is desirable when I am talking about God if I want to provoke people's curiosity (see Chapter 4). However, ambiguity should not be confused with uncertainty. Mrs Moore said in *A Passage to India*, 'I like mysteries but I dislike muddles.' It is only the confidence of my identity in Christ (Chapter 7) that makes me comfortable in using ambiguity to talk about my faith. The final chapter by Sara Savage looks at the different understandings of personhood behind the understanding of evangelism.

The thinking within this book can be located within four separate academic disciplines. The first is that of informal education. This, essentially, is the task of the youth worker –

11

informal education is an unstructured interaction with young people intended to promote critical awareness and reflective learning. There are five different strands to this type of education: commitment (i.e. what you want to achieve), context (how and where you meet with young people), conduct (appropriate behaviour), character (the role of personality), and conversation (what is said and how it is said). Within the discourse on informal education, *Ambiguous Evangelism* looks specifically at the role of conversation in talking about God.

The second discipline is theology and biblical studies. There are four different words used in the Bible that explain the idea of teaching: *didaxe*: an exegetical type of teaching, with the sense of 'instruction'; *exegesis*: a believer-to-believer type of teaching; *paraclesis*: an exhortatory type of teaching, typically used to encourage; *omilia*: an association or illustration of ideas. *Ambiguous Evangelism* builds primarily on the idea of *omilia*.

Third, the book has a grounding in sociology and, in Chapter 1, sociologist Sylvie Collins examines the empirical data that point to a prevailing national lack of awareness of the Christian faith.

Finally, within the discipline of psychology, Sara Savage writes about how the loss of religion is also the loss of an essential way of relating to and interpreting the human condition. Her chapter looks at how an understanding of God is a key to an understanding of self, and argues that without the knowledge of the Christian story people are deprived of a rich resource of self-realization and self-actualization.

1

The Sociological Context

Sylvie Collins

This chapter describes the decline in the salience and significance of Christian beliefs and practices in Britain over the last half century. As such it provides a general sociological context for the ideas presented in this book, a context in which fewer and fewer people attend church on a regular basis and large numbers of people are unfamiliar with the Christian story. The picture presented here is not unique to Britain. Western Europe generally has experienced a shift away from the traditions of the Church, particularly since the Second World War. Sociologists refer to this shift as the process of 'secularization'. This does not mean that individually people no longer believe in God or, indeed, the supernatural in general, but it does mean such beliefs are no longer controlled by the Church, and the Church as a social institution can no longer assume the authority and influence that it once had.

Danièle Hervieu-Léger (2000), writing about the situation in France, describes secularization as a loss of religious memory, by which she means there has been a loss of the particular way of believing and practising Christianity, which included legitimization of the faith by the authority of the Church and the passing on of a tradition from one generation to another down a lineage of believers. For Hervieu-Léger the Christian memory is, therefore, a collective one. Without the legitimating authority of the

Church to provide coherence and continuity, the memory is prone to disintegrate into a loose, subjective collection of beliefs, practices and symbols that are manipulated and reinterpreted according to individuals' personal preferences and agendas. As such, the memory mutates (Davie, 2000) and fades over successive generations. The aim of this chapter is to present an overview of the empirical evidence relating to Christianity in this country in order to provide a picture of where this process of secularization has left people's beliefs and practices in Britain today.

Church Attendance

The measures that are typically used by sociologists to gauge the significance of Christianity in people's lives are their religious affiliation, membership and attendance at church, and the kinds of attitudes and beliefs they subscribe to. These measures reveal a complex picture. In the 2001 Census, 72 per cent of the British population identified themselves as Christian. Yet the 1999 British Social Attitudes Survey found that only 46 per cent of people claimed a specific denominational membership (Table 1), and in terms of attendance just 15 per cent of those with, or brought up in, a religion attended church on a weekly or monthly basis (Table 2). As Tables 1 and 2 show, both of these measures were down on previous years.

Brierley's 1998 English Church Attendance Survey also suggests dwindling church attendance in that out of the population as a whole, only 7.5 per cent of people were to be found in church on an 'average' Sunday, compared to 10 per cent ten years earlier (Brierley, 2000), and most of these were older women (teenagers and men being particularly under-represented). Richter and Francis similarly note that an estimated 1,500 people leave churches each week (Richter and Francis, 1998:xii). And yet a large proportion of these church-leavers remain open to the possibility of returning to church at some point in the future (Richter and Francis, 1998). Church-leaving

Table 1. Church membership in Britain 1983–1999 (Jowell *et al.*, 2000:123)

Denomination	1983 %	1987 %	1991 %	1995 %	1999 %
Church of England	40	37	36	32	27
Roman Catholic	10	10	10	9	9
Church of Scotland	5	5	5	3	4
Other Protestant	7	7	6	6	6
Other religion	7	7	8	9	10
No religion	31	34	35	40	44
Base	*1,761*	*2,847*	*2,918*	*3,633*	*3,143*

Table 2. Church attendance (apart from such special occasions as weddings, funerals and baptisms) of those with a current religion or brought up in a religion 1991–1999 (Jowell *et al.*, 2000:124)

	1991 %	1995 %	1999 %
Once a week	12	13	13
At least every two weeks	3	3	2
At least once a month	7	6	6
At least twice a year	13	12	10
At least once a year	7	7	8
Less often	4	5	6
Never or practically never	51	55	54
Base	*2,687*	*3,333*	*2,834*

in itself does not necessarily mean a loss of Christian belief therefore, or indeed a hostility towards the Church at large: a finding confirmed by Jamieson's study of church-leaving in New Zealand (2002).

Openness to returning to church after leaving may reflect something of a life-cycle pattern in people's churchgoing practices:

children are taken to church by a parent, then leave during adolescence as part of the process of forming their own identity and world view, only to return again in adult life when they want to introduce their own children to religious and moral teaching. Increasingly, however, these life-cycle changes seem to be cross-cut by generational changes as well. These have been particularly noticeable since the 1960s.

The 1960s was the decade in which the post-war baby boomer generation came of age. It was a period of rapid social and political change. The Vietnam war, civil rights and feminist movements and, in particular, the expansion of higher education all raised young people's social and political awareness and caused them to challenge established patterns of social life and its institutions – including the Church. In this respect, the 1960s saw, among other things, the introduction of the contraceptive pill and more liberal divorce laws, both of which helped to free women to explore alternative life courses to those of domesticity and motherhood which had previously dominated their experiences. According to Brown (2001), these changes in women's life choices contributed to their moving away from the Church and finding their identity elsewhere. This was particularly significant for the decline of Christian memory, since it is women who are largely responsible for sustaining the faith on a day-to-day basis. Women are generally more religious than men in that they are more likely to pray, read the Bible and go to church. Indeed, they account for around 65 per cent of church attendance (Cameron, 2002). When women leave the Church, therefore, the consequences for the Christian memory can be severe.

The 1960s was also a relatively affluent time, which gave people a reasonably confident base from which to critique the establishment. New consumer markets were opening up and these provided goods and leisure activities that offered people alternative means of constructing and expressing their identity outside the main institutions. In this climate the Church appeared outdated and irrelevant to many people. Consequently, fewer people (particularly young people) associated themselves with it and many were less inclined to bring their own children up within the institutionalized faith. Bruce makes the point in relation to Sunday school attendance:

> ... at the start of the twentieth century half of Britain's children were socialized into Christian beliefs and doctrines. By the end of the century, the number of Sunday scholars was so small [around 4%] that either only the children of church-attenders went to Sunday school or not even all the children of regular churchgoers were being so socialized. (2002:68–9)

Indeed, Beaudoin's account of Generation X (the children of the baby boomers, born between 1960 and 1980) in the United States is reminiscent of the situation in Britain, and indicates that over the last 30 years popular culture, rather than the Church, has tended to provide young people with their spiritual nourishment and world view:

> During our lifetimes, especially during the critical period of the 1980s, pop culture was the amniotic fluid that sustained us. For a generation of kids who had a fragmented or completely broken relationship to 'formal' or 'institutional' religion, pop culture filled the spiritual gaps. (Beaudoin, 1998:21)

Attitudes towards the Church among young people in the 1990s (Generation Y) are no more positive than that of their parents. Leslie Francis's study of 33,000 13- to 15-year-olds (2001) revealed that 52 per cent of them thought church was boring, 28 per cent that it was irrelevant for life today, and 50 per cent that it was unnecessary insofar as they felt they could be a Christian without going to church. In my own research (Collins, 1997), some young people said they were also put off the Church because they felt it was hypocritical or out of touch with their lives. At the same time, however, Francis's study suggests that while there are some negative, indifferent or uncertain attitudes, most people are nevertheless glad that the Church is there and available to them should they need it, for example at times of major life events such as births, marriages and deaths. Thus, 73 per cent of the young people in Francis's survey said they would want to get married in church and 54 per cent that they would want their children baptized or christened there. This pattern holds for the adult population more generally.

Davie (2000) indicates that many parents who do not regularly go to church still want their babies baptized (approximately 50 per cent of children in Britain are baptized) and over 50 per cent of first marriages are marked by a religious ceremony. In this respect Davie (2000) argues that the Christian memory is held vicariously for the majority by the minority of churchgoers. This means that the memory is maintained for non-churchgoers so that they are able to tap into it on rare but significant life occasions and do not have to think too much about it the rest of the time. In this respect it is worth noting that the Church remains a powerful provider of ceremony and liturgy for people in Britain, particularly at a collective level (Davie, 2000).

Using Richter and Francis's study, Lings (2002) breaks down the British population into the following categories:

- 'regular attenders' (around 10 per cent of the population who attend a church on a weekly basis)
- 'fringe members' (approximately 10 per cent who attend one to three times every two months, but nevertheless see themselves as members)
- 'dechurched' (the 40 per cent who have had some experience of church but have now left; of whom around half are still open to returning at some point in their lives – the 'dechurched friendly')
- 'non-churched' or 'unchurched' (the remaining 40 per cent of people who very rarely or never have, or do, attend church – approximately 6 per cent of whom will be of other faiths).

This suggests that a large number of people profess a Christian faith but 'believe without belonging'.

Beliefs

So where does this leave belief? Very few people in Britain are atheists. The British Social Attitudes Survey suggests that only 10 per cent of people in 1998 definitely did not believe in God, 72 per cent had a belief in some sort of God or 'Higher Power' at least some of the time (see Tables 3 and 4).

Table 3. Belief in God in Britain, 1998 (taken from Jowell *et al.*, 2000:125)

Which statement comes closest to expressing what you believe about God?	1998 % agree
I don't believe in God	10
I don't know whether there is a God and I don't believe there is any way to find out	15
I don't believe in a personal God, but I believe in a Higher Power of some kind	14
I find myself believing in God some of the time, but not at others	14
While I have doubts, I feel I do believe in God	23
I know God really exists and I have no doubts about it	21
Base	*807*

Beliefs are not shared equally across the population, however. And just as there are differences in churchgoing according to age, so too are there differences in belief, with older people being more likely to subscribe to traditional Christian beliefs than younger people. The beliefs of the 13- to 15-year-olds in Francis's study are given in Table 5. These include a range of Christian and supernatural/spiritual ideas.

Several things can be noted from the figures given for young people in Table 5, which are confirmed in studies for adults too.

Table 4. Belief in a personal God (taken from Jowell *et al.*, 2000:126)

There is a God who concerns himself with every human being personally	1998 %
Agree strongly	10
Agree	19
Neither agree nor disagree	25
Disagree	20
Disagree strongly	12
Don't know	9
Base	*807*

Table 5. Christian and other beliefs (from Francis, 2001:36, 40)

	Yes %	Not certain %	No %
I believe in God	41	33	26
I believe that Jesus really rose from the dead	30	42	28
I believe in life after death	45	38	17
I believe God punishes people who do wrong	20	38	42
I think Christianity is the only true religion	16	37	47
I believe that God made the world in six days and rested on the seventh	20	40	40
I believe in the devil	22	28	51
I believe in my horoscope	35	29	36
I believe in ghosts	40	29	31
I believe in black magic	20	33	47
I believe that fortune-tellers can tell the future	20	30	50
I believe it is possible to contact the spirits of the dead	31	33	36

First, Christian beliefs have not disappeared altogether in many people's way of thinking. But, second, the extent of belief is relatively low and is selective in terms of traditional ideas. Thus, surveys tend to show people are more likely to believe in God than in the devil and in heaven than hell (see Table 6). Third, they also show that there is a great deal of uncertainty about traditional beliefs. In Table 5 around a third of young people simply do not know whether they believe in the ideas presented or not. This seems less the result of an unfinished spiritual quest than of simply not having thought through the beliefs in any great detail in the first place. Hornsby-Smith sums up the situation in his characterization of 'customary religion':

> . . . derived from 'official' religion but without being under its continuing control. . . . the beliefs and practices that make up customary religion are the product of formal religious socialisation but subject to trivialisation, conventionality, apathy, convenience and self-interest. (Hornsby-Smith, 1991:90)

Hornsby-Smith's statement draws attention to the fact that without being under the control of the Church ('official religion'), beliefs are free to become more subjective in content and interpretation. Gill (1999) makes the same point: churchgoing maintains belief; church-leaving diminishes belief. This is important because it suggests that the move away from churchgoing, noted above, is not simply the result of people losing their faith; church-leaving itself can cause a loss of faith. This is true even if the only time people go to church is involuntarily as children. In Table 6, using data from the 1991 British Social Attitudes Survey, Gill illustrates the difference in beliefs between adults who are totally unchurched (even during childhood) and those who have had some experience of church as children but have since left (the dechurched).

The dechurched are more likely than the unchurched to hold to Christian beliefs, even if they are no longer anchored in the tradition. This confirms Hervieu-Léger's argument; it seems that

Table 6. Faith in two groups of non-churchgoers – percentage who agree with the statement (taken from Gill, 1999:132–3)

	Non-churchgoers as children [*Unchurched*] (n = 126)	Weekly churchgoers as children [*Dechurched*] (n = 274)	Weekly sample (n = 1,206)
'I don't believe in God now and I never have'	40	6	12
'I believe in God now and I always have'	11	39	46
Never pray	70	41	32
Pray at least every fortnight	6	13	35
Strongly agree/agree that there is a God who concerns himself with every human being	4	18	32
Definitely/probably believe in:			
Life after death	31	35	47
Heaven	22	40	47
Hell	12	16	25
The devil	10	17	24
Religious miracles	12	26	38
Some faith healers	25	42	45

the Church is indeed important for sustaining and transmitting the faith, and as pressures of the modern world pull people away from the institution, so the memory fades.

Alternative Bearers of the Memory: Schools and the Media

For the unchurched in Britain there are, however, other institutional bearers of the Christian tradition that offer an echo of the memory and provide a baseline knowledge of the faith. Two significant examples are: religious education in schools, and the media (Davie, 2000).

Davie makes the point that nearly a quarter of all children in England and Wales are educated in denominational schools in the state system (Davie, 2000:85). Moreover, the 1988 Education Reform Act (following the 1944 Education Act) explicitly seeks to further the spiritual and moral development of young people in schools. This can happen in a variety of ways (for example, through the school ethos, its curriculum and acts of collective worship), but probably the most salient contributors to religious development for the majority of pupils are religious education classes and school assemblies.

Religious education in this country tends to be non-confessional in that its aim is to inform rather than convert. In this respect, the basic beliefs and practices of Christianity are taught so that young people at least have an awareness of the faith even if they do not directly engage with the tradition themselves. (A comparison can be made here with France where, as in Britain, church attendance is low, but in addition religious education is prohibited in schools. The consequence of this for French society has been the development of religious illiteracy among its young people [Davie, 2000:93]). However, while religious education may go some way to informing young people about Christianity, its non-confessional, information approach may end up simply relativizing its truth claims:

> Failing to take into account the truth claims of religions has two consequences. Practically it means that the teaching is confined to the externals of religions, their places of worship, their cult objects and their festivals. Their deeper beliefs which justify those places, objects and festivals are carefully avoided in case they raise truth claims. Such teaching can give the impression that religion is a superficial set of customs practised by those who happen to like them. More profoundly the avoidance of truth claims can suggest that no type of religion

can have any deep significance, nor lead to truth, and therefore that religious education is not an imperative study, and can be indoctrination into agnosticism. (Cox and Cairns, 1989:19).

In my own survey of just over 1,000 teenagers aged 13 to 16 years, young people's reactions to religious education in school were mixed. Thirty-one per cent said that they found religious education lessons interesting, but interview comments revealed that classes were not always taken very seriously. Twenty-two per cent agreed that religious education lessons helped them form their religious beliefs, but many felt that religious education was best suited to those who were already 'religious' and should not be compulsory for the rest. Some comments from the young people who did have a Christian faith echoed Cox and Cairns' point above in that they felt school religious education lessons compromised their faith.

In addition to religious education classes, the 1988 Education Reform Act requires schools to hold a daily act of collective worship which, over the course of a term, is predominantly Christian. This is a tall order for any school to follow and, indeed, expects a higher degree of religious practice from children than is exercised by most adults in this country. In terms of maintaining a Christian memory, there are pros and cons to collective worship in schools. On the one hand, it does provide an opportunity to introduce young people to the practice of prayer, to articulate parts of the Christian story in a devotional context, and to learn aspects of church practice such hymn-singing. On the other hand, many young people find worship, particularly in school assemblies, boring, irrelevant or embarrassing (Collins, 1997). In this situation there is always the danger that the young people will generalize unfavourable experiences of worship in school to other contexts, including church services, thereby putting them off from considering the tradition further. Given the above, it is perhaps not surprising that the head of Ofsted, David Bell, has recently suggested the requirement for daily worship in schools be reduced to weekly or monthly worship (BBC *News*, 21 April 2004).

Similarly, the media also maintain the Christian tradition – up to a point. Terrestrial television and BBC radio as part of its public service mandate provide both devotional and religious documentary programmes. Davie (2000:106) makes the point that hymn-singing programmes are still fairly popular. A large proportion of the audience is elderly, however, and grew up in a churchgoing culture so that such activities are familiar. Whether these programmes will continue to be broadcast in the future remains to be seen given the generational shifts already noted. An Ofcom consultation on public service broadcasting does not bode well (Ofcom, 2004). It found that when audiences were asked to rate 17 programme types in terms of value to themselves and their family and for the good of society, religious programmes were placed second to last. Top of the list for personal value came news and drama programmes, while top of the list for social good were news and sport.

Apart from religious broadcasting, Davie argues that the mass media (particularly newspapers) can have the effect of helping to ensure the Church acts as a proper guardian of the Christian tradition. This is because they perform a surveillance function whereby any improprieties on the part of the Church and its officials are subject to vicious headlines and comment. This perhaps testifies to the importance of the Church in the public's mind, but such reporting does tend to undermine the credibility of the Church in the long term (McDonnell, 2003).

However, the media's relationship to religion is complex, and indeed produces a range of diverse and at times conflicting messages. At the same time as supporting some aspects of the Christian memory, it also undermines it by trivializing the Church – as, for example, when the comedy programme *Father Ted* gently pokes fun at the Catholic Church, or when television dramas and soap operas portray religious people as slightly strange or odd in some way – and by providing competing ideas, particularly in terms of what has been labelled 'new age' spiritualities. Many newspapers and magazines carry articles on mind, body and spirit practices designed to restore inner peace to the soul and outer harmony to people's lives. Indeed, in December 2003 *Cosmopolitan* magazine appointed a spirituality editor to guide its readers through the array of spiritual choices now on offer (aromatherapy, reflexology, crystals, astrology, etc.). These practices sometimes have loose connections with one or other of the existing world faiths (including Christianity), but their ideas and symbols are disembedded from tradition and reinterpreted in such a way that they become individualized forms of spirituality, and potentially cults in their own right. Richards (2003), for instance, describes the current fascination with angels in popular culture as a case in point. In this respect, religious awareness in Britain has broadened out into a more generalized notion of spirituality, and become something of a consumer choice and leisure pursuit.

For some Christians the salience of new age ideas in popular culture has introduced the fear that alternative spiritualities will lead people away from Christianity. There have been concerns among more conservative Christian groups, for example, that the depiction of magic and the supernatural in books and films such as the *Harry Potter* series and *Lord of the Rings* will tempt young people into studying the occult (Ostling, 2003). It is difficult to get substantial empirical evidence of the extent to which this may be happening because, while new age and occult books and products are becoming increasingly available to people on the high street, it is hard to tell how they are used on a day-to-day basis and how seriously they are taken. Lynda Woodhead and her colleagues in Lancaster have, perhaps, come closest to researching the significance of alternative spiritualities (or, as they call it, the 'holistic milieu') in people's lives, with a fairly exhaustive examination of the public uptake of new age practices in the market town of Kendal. Out of a population of about 28,000 people, they found only around 2 per cent were involved with alternative practices which they, the practitioners, felt to be 'spiritual' (most of whom were middle-aged women), compared to nearly 8 per cent of people who were regular church attenders (Woodhead, 2004; see also Heelas *et al.*, 2004). There are two important points to take from this. First, that the holistic milieu has not yet over-taken the Church as a source of spiritual practice and, second, there are in this case study 25,000 people left unaccounted for by either church or alternative spirituality involvement. It is these 25,000 that seem to represent the bulk of people in Britain.

Looking specifically at the effect of *Harry Potter* and its genre in popular culture, there is also little evidence that large numbers of young people are taking up magic or occult practices. This is partly because young people are highly media-literate and are not easily taken in by its constructions (Savage, Collins and Mayo, 2003; Allan, 1995) and partly because, as with the Christian story, they have little broader knowledge of the occult onto which to hang these new ideas. Indeed, Ostling (2003) argues it is precisely because *Harry Potter* does not rely on such a knowledge, but rather on more familiar science-based calculability, that the stories are so popular:

> . . . magic as historically practised has depended on networks of meaning and metaphor and on a lively sense, indeed experience, of the world as being full of spirits, forces, and agentival powers, whereas Harry Potter's magic presupposes a universe governed by impersonal causality.
>
> . . . I would suggest that Harry Potter is popular *because* his magic is disenchanted, because he makes the extraordinary ordinary, and therefore, familiar and unchallenging. (Ostling, 2003:10, 16)

As with the relativizing of faith through non-confessional religious education, the main danger for Christianity from the media probably lies less in the alternatives it presents, than in the fact that, by giving so many alternatives, the plausibility of any one of them as a description of ultimate truth is severely undermined (Bruce, 1996).

A Fading Memory

In sum, the British context seems to be one in which most people are broadly sympathetic to Christian beliefs and, indeed, the Church. Thus when people think about religion at all, the vast majority still think in terms of Christianity and many look to the Church to provide a liturgical expression for major life events. But the vast majority of the British population are dechurched or unchurched, and the Christian faith does not have a consciously-felt impact on most people for most of the time. Indeed, studies indicate that generally people give relatively little thought to matters of ultimate or transcendent significance on a day-to-day basis, and tend to live their lives in terms of more immediate realities (Cottrell, 1985). My own research into young people's faith indicated that it was personal relationships with family and friends and the pursuit of self-fulfilment and happiness in the material world that formed the framework around which they made sense of their daily lives. When matters of ultimate concern, such as birth or death, occasionally penetrated normal life and more immediate loci of meaning were insufficient to explain events, the young people generally turned to Christianity as their back-up system; but there was little sense of the faith tradition which lay behind the beliefs and practices to which they turned – there were just echoes of the memory. And yet the young people in my study felt that they knew enough about the faith to meet their needs, and there was very little evidence of their wanting to search for a deeper understanding.

The Church has to some extent recognized that the Christian memory is fading away and evangelistic initiatives have been taken specifically to re-member the story. The *Alpha* course is perhaps the most well known of the more recent initiatives specifically targeted at unchurched people. It aims to re-present the basic teachings of the faith (at least a charismatic evangelical version of it) to those who have forgotten or never come across them in the first place. The success of *Alpha* in accomplishing this has yet to be fully and independently assessed. However, one

28

interesting finding in a study by Hunt (2003) is that the *Alpha* course tends to attract those already in the church or on its fringes. Some people come to the course wanting to deepen their faith, while others want to revise the basics. It is perhaps a worrying thought that even churchgoers feel their understanding of Christianity is inadequate. Yet relatively few of the unchurched population have attended *Alpha* courses. It is for this reason that other ways of communicating the faith need to be developed to sit alongside *Alpha* and its equivalents. It is hoped that the ideas presented in this book will be a helpful contribution to this task.

2

Generation Y

———⊰∘⊱———

This book draws on the conclusions of a recent two-year UK research project that looked via the popular arts at the world view of young people born after 1980 (known as 'Generation Y'). The empirical research comes from a project originally initiated by Theology Through the Arts (Cambridge and St Andrews) and funded by the Mercers' Company of London. I am very grateful to both organizations for their support. This project was undertaken by Dr Sara Savage (CARTS, Faculty of Divinity, University of Cambridge Centre; myself, Revd Dr Bob Mayo (Centre for Youth Ministry, Ridley Hall); and Dr Sylvie Collins (Dept of Sociology, University of Kingston), and is now a forthcoming Church House publication: *Post-secular Spirituality: Young People's Worldview via the Popular Arts* (Savage, Collins and Mayo). I refer here to the research findings insofar as they substantiate the central thesis of this book: that there is an essential lack of knowledge about the Christian faith in a growing percentage of the population.

The Significance of World Views

The purpose of our research was not to uncover an aesthetic appreciation of popular art and culture, but to understand how young people's interaction with popular art and culture shaped their world view.

Everybody has a world view that is, to some degree, shared with others in society through 'culture'. Understanding someone's world view is tantamount to understanding their perception of themself. World views provide the taken-for-granted assumptions that shape how we think about the world around us. To use an analogy, a world view is like a pair of spectacles through which we view the world, rather than what we see with those spectacles – change the spectacles and we see the world in a different way.

A world view embraces all deep-level human perceptions of reality, how a person perceives their role within the society and their relationship to the world. World views are the conceptual frameworks through which people make sense of their lives; they provide the stories through which people view reality. They contain basic beliefs about 'how the world is' and 'how the world should be'; they include ideas about where individuals belong in society, what values they hold dear, what goals are worth aspiring to and so on. The concept of a world view can provide a way of listening to and interpreting what young people say about themselves. To appreciate a young person's world view is to get a glimpse of how they see themselves as relating to the rest of the world.

This is what our youth and world view research did by looking at young people's responses to various forms of popular art and culture. The research was based on a series of 26 interviews with groups of young people, mainly aged between 15 and 25. The choice of genres on which to focus arose out of Wright's (1992) thinking about world views. Wright (1992:123) suggests that world views are articulated through stories (the myths and narratives that explain who we are, where we are and why we are the way we are, etc.), symbols (which articulate and represent the meaning of the stories) and praxis (rituals and practices that embody the meaning of the stories). In our research, story was represented by soap operas and films. The interviewees were asked to talk generally about films and British soap operas they had seen. They were also questioned specifically on how they might deal with an issue if they were in the shoes of one of the *EastEnders* characters. For symbol, the interview groups were asked to look at and comment on a series of 16 advertising and cultural images, chosen to reflect a range of existential issues. They were then asked to select an image that resonated with them and to explain the reasons for their choice. Praxis was interpreted as contemporary genres of pop music (dance, R&B, garage, house) and the young people's experiences of clubbing.

The project met with 26 different groups of young people, aged mainly between 15 and 25, in colleges/universities and youth clubs across the country. The sample of young people reflected some of the main demographic characteristics of English youth. Nineteen groups were mixed gender, four were single-sex male and three single-sex female. In total 135 young people took part in the study. Of these 52 per cent were female, 48 per cent male; 94 per cent were White, 6 per cent Black or Asian; 60 per cent defined themselves as non-Christian, 40 per cent as Christian. The youngest persons interviewed were 13 (7 young people). The oldest person was 30 (1 person). The modal age was 17 with a mean of 18 years and three months. Four of the interview sites were among students in higher education and 14 sites were from youth and community work projects.

Each group was audio-recorded and the data transcribed. At the end of the process there were around 500 pages of transcribed material; our qualitative analysis was conducted with the aid of N4 Classic computer software. A strength of our work together was that we were a cross-disciplinary research team – Sara's background discipline is psychology; Sylvie's background discipline is sociology and I come from the world of informal education and theology. There were two field trips to night clubs where people were asked to give their best and worst experience of clubbing and to describe anything extraordinary that had happened to them while clubbing.

There was also a questionnaire posted on different clubbing websites, and the *EastEnders* message board was monitored throughout the research period. The interviewees did not represent the most excluded young people in society. This in part reflected the nature of our research, which pertained to the socially shared (and therefore inclusive) world view that arose from consumption and immersion in pop culture. Being a consumer of popular culture presupposes 'inclusion' to some extent in that participation at least requires a home equipped with a television, sound system or Walkman, and disposable income and leisure.

Ignorant, but Happy

Two distinctive themes within Generation Y were confirmed by our youth and world view research. The first of these was the lack of knowledge about the Christian faith. The second was that the world view of the interviewees was generally happy and positive.

There was little evidence of people drawing on Christian religious concepts to frame their thinking and response to a situation. There was also limited evidence of people looking for others to provide external information or direction to help them to reach decisions about what to do. Religious and supernatural symbols had little resonance among them – all the more striking given that 40 per cent of the participants identified themselves as Christian. An image of Buffy holding a stake to slay vampires and tackle the forces of evil produced no spiritual or supernatural echoes for the young people: the responses were 'this worldly', rather than 'other worldly'. Young men fancied her and young women considered her as a powerful female role model – in other words the females wanted to be like her and the men wanted her.

In two pilot focus groups, Dali's painting of Christ crucified was presented to the interviewees, along with a Hubble telescope picture of the night sky. The expectation had been that these might trigger some form of religious or spiritual response. However, neither image connected with the interviewees in any significant way, and both images were subsequently dropped. The conclusion was that interviewees did not have the religious knowledge to connect with the image of the crucifixion, nor was there an inclination to wonder at the night sky.

These images were replaced with others we considered to be more provocative, among them, an image of the comedian Ali G posing on a cross. There was one strand of reaction that was traditional and conservative. However, it appeared that the young people were not defending religion so much as the idea of religion. They were happy for the Church to have a role providing it did not inconvenience them. On the occasions when this was connected in the interviewees' minds with the figure of Jesus, this got a conservative reaction. It was considered to be 'mocking' or 'offensive'. One of the images used was the Benetton advertisement of the face of Jesus superimposed onto a man dying of Aids. The interviewees who recognized this as such reacted strongly and questioned the right of Benetton to use the advert in this way. A comment made was, 'What the hell has it got to do with Benetton? . . . really bad.'

Their complaint against Benetton could have been as much to do with the use of a dying man as the use of the face of Jesus. Either way, it is illustrative of an equally conservative reaction to the image. Other instances of traditional and conservative reactions to stimuli included, both with images and with *EastEnders*, a positive response to traditional gender stereotyping and roles. Also, one group responded to images of September 11th, 2001 entirely in terms of how it might affect their prospects in the job market.

The second, perhaps more surprising, significant feature to emerge from our youth and world view research was that the interviewees in general seemed happy. The study identified a coherent narrative, which could be encapsulated as: this world, and all life in it, is meaningful as it is; there is no need to think of significance as being somewhere else. Implicit in this world view, for which Sara Savage coined the phrase 'happy midi-narrative',[1] is the belief that the universe and the social world are essentially benign. Although difficult things do happen in life, there are enough resources within the individual and their family and friends to enable happiness to prevail. Happiness is the goal of life. As one young person said, 'Happiness is the ideal you aim for.'

It is understood that one person's happiness should not exclude another's. The scope of this communal happiness, however, is modest: it pertains mainly to 'me, my family and my friends'; the narrative is lived out on a 'midi' scale. This echoes previous research which has identified that the new emerging generation wants to have a good time – whether that means playing computer games or clubbing the night away – as the *Evening Standard* put it, having it all is seen as a right not a luxury (*Evening Standard*, 11 October 2002).

One of the findings of the research, therefore, was that people feel generally happy and are not feeling the lack of religion; people don't miss what they do not know.

Forms of Spirituality

Our youth and world view research puts flesh on the idea of a fading Christian memory discussed in Chapter 1. It also offers insight into the idea that a decline in church attendance and a depletion of a Christian knowledge base has triggered a subsequent rise in transcendent spiritualities (traditional or alternative) among young people. The indication from the research, however, was that a decline in religion has not been balanced by a rise in spirituality.

I suggest that the view which would see an increase in spiritual hunger corresponding to a decline in church significance relies on making unsubstantiated general conclusions out of specific instances. For example, Lynch (2002) talks about the possibility of a clubbing spirituality (a connectedness that comes from a group experience in the sense of being a part of being something bigger). The clubbing spirituality described by Lynch, though, is among older people (Generation X) who have looked in the Church, found it wanting, and are now looking elsewhere. And there are some younger people who will look for meaning and purpose within the Church, be put off by church structures, and then look for meaning, purpose and self-expression in other places. Jamieson (2002) has also documented the phenomenon of people leaving the church but continuing to hold to their Christian beliefs. But the fact that there is a group of people identified as disillusioned with the Church and looking elsewhere for meaning and expression does not by any means signify an inherent spiritual longing within the general population. Inevitably there are going to be instances of 'designer spirituality' within groups of post-Church people: people who have sampled the Church's approach now looking to frame their spiritual convictions in a more individualistic manner. But it is not possible to infer from this that there is an inbuilt 'God-searching gene' in everyone, that will seek expression elsewhere if it cannot find a home in the Church.

It is true that with the collapse of the established-Church state religion and the disappearance of a shared Christian religious narrative, people are free to shape their own ideas and use words such as 'spirituality' in any way they want – as the Ministry of Sound did when they brought out a double CD entitled *The Karma Collection* (limited edition of spiritual chill-out vibes featuring Panjabi MC, Jakatta, Letfield, Moby, Koop, Oakenfield, Bent). On Saturdays, *The Times* includes a magazine entitled *Body and Soul*. This can contain, for example (24 February 2004), articles on forgiving an alcoholic parent, yoga in Morocco and a review of different types of shaving foams and gels. I am equally able to describe myself as being involved in a spiritual activity whether I am soaking in aromatherapy bath oils, drinking organic carrot juice or going to church. Jemima Hunt wrote in the *Financial Times* (20 December 2003) that where traditional religion's star is waning, that of designer spiritualism is 'spectacularly in the ascendant'. She suggested that despite our illiteracy in the Christian story, we have not lost our religious – or rather spiritual – sensibilities. However, this 'soul shopping', which she referred to as being as popular among women as shoe shopping, is not, as she suggests, despite our illiteracy in the Christian story but because of it. This is because there is so little underpinning religious knowledge that people can use the word 'spiritual' to mean whatever they want.

Any term is debased if it is used too widely and this is true of the use of the word 'spirituality'. The various meanings of 'spirituality' can be categorized into two broad types. The first is theological in that it includes some underlying awareness of a deeper purpose or motivation for day-to-day living. In crude terms, this would be an understanding of the transcendent expressed through an organized framework (e.g. going to church). Theological spirituality would emphasize the reaction of the individual to the revelation of God through Jesus Christ. Dykstra (1981) talked of an appropriate and intentional participation in the redemptive activity of Christ. The second use of the word 'spirituality' is personal. Personal spirituality, in contrast, puts more emphasis on the individual person making sense of their lives. When the band U2 sing 'I still haven't found what I am looking for', or Jameilia sings about how much she learnt through an abusive relationship, it is spirituality in this personal sense, in that it is a searching for meaning rather than an acknowledgement of transcendence.

Personal spirituality is essentially an existential term referring to the meaning-making, pattern-forming, significance-giving aspect of a person's life. In this respect, going clubbing or snowboarding could be described as a spiritual activity insofar as the individual is electing to do that rather than some other activity; the chosen activity is then providing them with value and purpose. It is, however, a reductive view of spirituality in which religious experience often simply is recast as the human emotion of a peak experience, in some cases barely distinguishable from the exhilaration of a bungee jump or some other form of extreme physical activity.

It is this sense of spirituality that applies when it is suggested that activities such as clubbing qualify as 'spiritual'. There is clearly a personal spirituality inherent in clubbing in the sense that clubbers are participating in an activity that is giving purpose, value and significance to the rest of their week. But clubbing does not have an inherent theological spirituality

37

because clubbers are not participating in an activity that is giving them either an automatic understanding or an experience of God. The Church has sold the family silver if, in classifying a night's clubbing as 'spiritual', it is suggesting that the clubbing experience contains within it the transformative potential of a religious encounter. To put it crudely – if someone is 'getting off their head' in a club, then they are simply 'getting off their head' in a club. It is an experience of self, rather than an experience of God.

There are two objections that might be raised over this reading of the use of the term 'spirituality'. The first is that someone's experience of God need not be limited to a church, and God can be experienced at 4 a.m. in a club in the same way that God can be experienced anywhere else. However, the conclusion from our youth and world view research was that there has been an element of wish-fulfilment from the Christian constituency, who want to read an awareness of God into what is essentially nothing more than an extreme type of experience. A theological spirituality through clubbing may be the reported experience of some Christian young people, but this is because they are interpreting the clubbing experience within their pre-held theological framework. A Christian young person will experience God because of what they take into, rather than because of what they take out of, the clubbing experience.

A second possible objection is that there is not a clear distinction between the two types of spirituality, and one can lead into the other. Indeed, it seems evident that theological spirituality will involve an expression of personal spirituality, since value-forming can be assumed as a part of a belief in God. However, there is no conclusive evidence for the reverse – despite the fact that God or religion is sometimes mentioned explicitly in the lyrics of songs. *Faithless* (1998) sang about how God was a DJ and the club was a church. *Pink* (2004) followed on singing that if God was a DJ, then life was the dance floor.

The fact that these songs use the word 'church' to describe the clubbing experience does not mean that it is making a like-for-like comparison with the Sunday-by-Sunday gathering of Christian believers. Rather, the comparison lies in the idea of a gathered community in a church and an emoted community in clubbing where all that matters is the dancing and the music. Both *Faithless* and *Pink*'s songs were written to enhance the clubbing experience rather than to express any conviction about God – the *Faithless* song is a flippant rave tune by a '30-something' Generation X band. Even though both songs use religious imagery, it does not automatically mean that they are expressing a belief in God. Instead the religious imagery is being used to give a heightened significance to the night's clubbing. In the case of clubbing, it seems likely that the personal spirituality is entirely self-contained; after all, it is the extreme nature of the experience that provides its significance in the clubber's week.

Religious Awareness Within Popular Culture

Clearly different uses of the term 'spirituality' have resulted in some confusion over what it actually means. This idea is echoed by the insights of Beaudoin (1998), who was intrigued by the fact that Generation X-ers (born between 1960 and 1980) were hostile toward religion or dismissive of it, and yet they still claimed to be 'spiritual'. Beaudoin (1998) identified among Generation X-ers a suspicion of institutions (especially organized religion) and a significance given to personal experience. He looked for a dialogue between religious institutions and the popular culture of Generation X-ers.

Beaudoin (2003:18) wrote that one of the most common ways for people of faith to describe themselves today is as a 'spiritual' person (as distinct from 'religious' person). Someone's spirituality may be their way of talking about faith in a deity, in nature, in a particular value or in themselves. However, he admitted that, according to the faith to which this spirituality refers, there is no person without faith in something or someone. If anything can be described as potentially spiritual, then the word loses any distinctive meaning so that spirituality referring to anything ends up as spirituality meaning nothing.

Our youth and world view research suggests that there are two significant differences between the two viewpoints of Beaudoin (1998) and Beaudoin (2003). The first is that the dialogue between church institutions and popular culture has not happened, therefore the uses of the word 'spirituality' have continued to multiply without being anchored in any religious discourse. 'Spirituality', as Beaudoin (2003) admitted, can now be used to describe anything from individualistic self-fulfilment to a searching after and realization of God. The point of this book is that a natural inquisitiveness and a desire to make sense of experience is not necessarily the same as a longing for God. The second difference is that the religious knowledge base of Generation Y (born after 1981) has decreased to the extent that there is less of the automatic hostility towards organized religion that Beaudoin (1998) had observed. There are many people who are not and never have been in a position of deciding how to react to the figure of Jesus. It has simply never occurred to them that there is something to respond to.

Religious jewellery, for example, is often worn not as a reaction against the Church but with a self-contained, self-defining significance. I asked a waitress at a busy north London eatery whether the cross that she was wearing was a just a piece of jewellery or whether it was a statement of a belief. She replied, proudly, that it was a gift from her boyfriend and she had not taken it off since he had given it to her. It was a meaningful, significant and important piece of jewellery, but in her mind it had nothing to do with the events of a crucifixion 2,000 years previously. The same point is made by the fabled story about the lady buying a necklace: when a shop assistant asked her what kind of pendant she wanted, she replied, 'A silver cross,' then added, 'the one with the little man on it.'

Within popular culture there have been deliberate references to the Christian faith that are clearly connected to the Christian story. These can be read either as affirmation of or reaction against the Christian faith. Examples include some of Madonna's songs in the 1980s and Michael Jackson's imitation of Christ at the 1996 Brit Awards. After his performance of 'Earthsong' he was dressed in a dazzling white outfit, hoisted over the stage in a crucifixion pose, and surrounded by children and a rabbi reaching to touch him. Jarvis Cocker was so incensed at the way Jackson was portraying himself as some Christ-like figure with the power of healing that he invaded the stage in protest. In 1998, Lauryn Hill accepted the Grammy Album of the Year award by reading a passage from Psalm 40, adding, 'Know that God is great and he conquers all.' However, Madonna, Michael Jackson and Lauryn Hill all come out of a religious background, and this is recognized as giving a context for their actions.

There are also allusions to the Christian faith that cannot be connected so immediately with the Christian story. It is easy to read significance into the fact that there is a messianic quest for what is real in the *Matrix* movies or that Philip Pullman's *His Dark Materials* trilogy with its analysis of religious truth and power has become a bestseller with a sell-out stage version at the National Theatre in London. These things cannot be taken to mean though that there is an open public debate on religion. The presence of religious themes in popular culture, I would argue, does not in itself imply an engagement with the Christian story; music videos showing religious iconography, for example, are often simply a manipulation of cultural artefacts rather than a deliberate expression of conviction. It could also be argued that this type of trivialization is of less benefit to the Church than deliberate blasphemy, which would at least indicate a common frame of reference and a desire to engage.

A common mistake made by the Christian constituency is to assume that comments or actions are contingent upon certain attitudes or beliefs. Examples of potentially misleading instances to trap the unwary abound:

- When the carol 'Silent night' was played in Starbucks before Christmas, it was not an indication of Christian awareness, just seasonal musical wallpaper.

- At a church youth group in north London, the members decided to paint their names onto their hands next to a logo of the cross. When asked why they had chosen to do this, they replied that it was the logo of the club. Thus, even belonging to a church youth group and drawing a cross onto their hands could not be interpreted as a statement of belief in this particular case. To these young people the cross was nothing more than the corporate logo of the youth club, a statement of identity on the same sort of level as the Nike swoosh.

- My *Bob the Builder* chocolate advent calendar ran up until 31 December rather than 25 December, but this was not a deliberate attempt to marginalize Christmas. Rather, it simply made good commercial sense to charge more money for a calendar with six more days to open – and consequently six more chocolates. A Kylie Minogue version called itself a *Count Down Calendar* and went up to 1 January, which seems not so much a case of ignoring Christmas as never having recognized it in the first place.

- Smokers with a conscience can now buy an ashtray with 'Jesus Hates Smoking' printed on the base. It might look like commerce kicking out against religion, but in reality indicates nothing more than a business decision about what is expected to sell. I can go into Paperchase and choose from a Jesus action figure ('with poseable arms and gliding action') and a dashboard Jesus with a spring and an adhesive base ('enlightenment on a spring')! Neither are marketed nor understood as anti-religious, but simply as cultural icons that are expected to sell. It is not disrespect but cultural appropriation that puts Jesus on sale as an action man figure at £4.99.

- Vibe FM, a local radio station in Cambridgeshire and Suffolk, ran a phone poll to find out whether people preferred New Year or Christmas celebrations. The voting was 52 per cent in favour of Christmas – on the basis that it was more fun to have the children included. The discussion was simply over which party was more fun, and the reasons behind the respective celebrations did not enter the discussion. The evening of

42

Good Friday, according to Vibe FM listeners, is Bank Holiday Friday Girls' Night Out: come dressed in combat gear for a night banging out the music and 'doing it large'. There was no acknowledgement that Good Friday was a central day in the Christian Church's liturgical year.

- Staying with kitsch, NookArt – wholesaler of 'Funky Fashion Jewellery, Beaded and Flower Door Curtains, the Kitsch Switch, Trendy Lamps and Much More' – sells a Jesus Super Hero (JSH) 'who comes with wheels 'cos he's wheely good'.

There is a theological response and a sociological response that can be made to a Jesus Super Hero figure (JSH) who 'comes with wheels 'cos he's wheely good'. The theological response is that the central Christian symbol of belief is the image of the crucified Christ. The crucifixion was an act of misunderstanding the figure of Christ; hence the central symbol of belief is that of a misunderstood man. The NookArt Christ suggests that this misunderstanding, albeit in a different way, continues. The sociological response is that there are enough free-floating pieces of religious information in people's minds to make the Jesus Super Hero figure interesting enough for them to purchase. The Ship of Fools website parodies this interest in religious artefacts by displaying a selection of the religious kitsch available. Choice items include the Virgin Mary or communion fridge magnet set, a 12 apostles pewter beer mug, a Virgin Mary memo board, 'wash away your sins' soap, a 'Jesus hates it when you smoke' ashtray, a 'new born again glucosamine super pain relieving' formula, a pet baptismal kit, a 'now is the time to repent' wristwatch, a frisbee of faith and a praying teddy.

The nativity play put on at my local primary school, in the middle of the politically correctly named Winterfest season, was called *Who? What? Why? Where? When?* The programme notes informed me that:

the story begins when two time travellers arrive on planet earth in the 21st century; their mission is to find the true meaning of Christmas. Little do they know where their search will take them.

However even this play, with its supposedly clear statement of intent, was simply a seasonal activity and not an expression of belief. It is quite acceptable for a nativity play to include reindeer, or even (in the film *Love Actually*) lobsters, simply to cater for the number of children who need a part to play. Even the *Sun* newspaper will reflect the seasonal mood by including the Christmas story by text.

> N lo, * wich they saw
> in east, wnt b4 it
> stpd wear yng kid wos.
> wen they saw *, they
> wer wel ☺ n wen they
> cum they saw yng kid
> wi Mary is mam, n fel
> dwn, n worshipd im. N
> wen they ad opnd ther
> stuff, they give un2 im
> gfts of Au, frank and mir
>
> Evry 1 wos wel hapy
> and ad a masiv prty n
> from that day on it was
> cald xmas.
>
> Amn
> Mark Bowness, *Sun*, 29 November 2003

A recognition of the extent of the depletion of the knowledge base of Christianity will involve a shift in the self-perception of the Christian constituency. If it is believed that people are consciously choosing to exclude themselves from an active participation in the Christian faith, then the implication is that people have reacted against what they have heard. This can lead to an implicit assumption on behalf of the Christian constituency that since the Church's presentation has been tried and found wanting, then there must be either an inbuilt apathy or an inbuilt hostility towards the gospel. But assuming that society is inherently hostile to the Church is the same mistake as assuming that they are inherently curious.

A friend of mine was explaining the struggle she had to convince her teenage daughter that if she and her husband ever argued then, in all probability, it had nothing to do with her as their daughter. 'Your mother and father', she would explain, 'have their own separate lives and it is not your responsibility to sort out any disagreement between the two of us; equally you must not assume that any disagreement is necessarily about you.' This conversation illustrates the extent to which people will interpret events according to how they affect them when, in all reality, they may equally well have nothing to do with them at all. In the same way, the Christian constituency can assume that people are reacting against the Church when all too often they are not taking the Church into consideration.

It is illogical to assume that someone is reacting against something of which they are not even aware, and generally people are not deciding against coming to church; more often it has simply never occurred to them to do so in the first place. However, this perception of being declined feeds into the Christian psyche in an expectation that people will automatically be hostile to any proclamation of the Christian faith. Fernando (2001) wrote that the whole world is growing in its hostility to the doctrine of the uniqueness of Christ. Perceptions such as these are absorbed into the Christian's sense of identity; after all, this is no more than what was promised in the Gospels: 'All men will hate you because of me' (Matthew 10.22). This reference, however, is specific to Jesus' sending out of the 12 disciples. The idea that the Church is waging war not against flesh and blood but against the principalities and powers (2 Corinthians 10.3) is not an adequate rationale to assume that people will automatically be hostile to discussion of the Christian faith. Generally, while conducting the youth and world view research programme I was met, at worst, with a slightly jaded, 'take it or leave it' or 'what have you got to offer?' attitude from the young people. There was no unease or hostility to my making an enquiry about the Christian faith.

This same supposition that there is in society an inbuilt dislike of Christianity was echoed in the Christmas 2003 address of Dr Rowan Williams, the Archbishop of Canterbury, when he said that it isn't all that surprising if a secular environment looks at religion not only with suspicion or incomprehension but also with fear. The idea underlying the Archbishop's statement is that people view Christianity with hostility because they see Christianity as having a past to live down; he referred to the fact that religion had too often become the language of the powerful and an excuse for oppression. It is true that people with an understanding of Christianity may be hostile or suspicious, but people without an understanding will be neither. The reality of the contemporary context is that while some people will react with hostility or suspicion to the Christian message, some people will be reacting with indifference because they are not aware enough of it in the first place.

The BBC marked the twenty-fifth anniversary of the pontificate of Pope John Paul II and the beatification of Mother Teresa with a documentary about the effectiveness of condoms in the fight against Aids. Mario Conti, the Archbishop of Glasgow, accused the corporation of 'rudeness', 'prejudice', 'gross insensitivity' and an 'anti-Catholic bias'. It is unclear to me, though, whether this programme planning was, as Archbishop Conti suggested, hostility, or whether it was simply indifference.

People cannot be said to be reacting with hostility or suspicion to something that does not have a reality for them in the first place. The 'unchurched' person does not know enough about the faith to blame the Church for its chequered past. They are not reacting against or rejecting the Christian faith. They are simply not aware of the Christian faith as an eternal truth and a potential life option. The dwindling stock of Christian knowledge means that when the Christian message is introduced, people will as often respond out of curiosity and interest rather than out of fear, suspicion or hostility.

Implications

A person's first thoughts on a subject tend to become defining ideas, which then colour every subsequent new idea they encounter. I demonstrated this fact to a student group by asking how they would react to me if they had been told, by a third party, that I was in the habit of beating my wife. It would not matter how good a lecturer I was, I would for ever be cast in their minds as someone who beat his wife. However, my mother will always see me as her son – and nothing else: when I moved to my current teaching post she expressed amazement that the college had given me a whole lecture room to myself and that students would want to come and listen to what I had to say. The findings of the research suggest that even when a Christian feels that they have been clear in speaking about their Christian faith, this is not necessarily how it has been perceived by someone 'unchurched', who does not have an adequate structure of interpretation. This is because the unchurched person's presuppositions affect the way they hear the Christian's discourse.

New information is interpreted in the light of existing knowledge. This means that 'Jesus Christ' can either be heard as a swear word or as the name of the Son of God. It depends on the context and the perception of the person talking. Paul talked about focusing on what is pure, lovely and admirable on the basis that what one finds in a person is always decided by what one is looking for: 'Whatever is true, whatever is noble, whatever is right, whatever is pure, whatever is lovely, whatever is admirable – if anything is excellent or praiseworthy – think about such things' (Philippians 4.8–9).

A weatherman will look at the sky and see troughs and peaks and wind flows; I will look at the sky and see nothing more than clouds. A builder will look at a wall and see whether it is a hollow stud partitioned wall as opposed to solid brick; I will look at the wall and see nothing more than bricks. A Christian will look at the world and see sin, redemption and salvation; a person without the underlying Christian narrative will look at the world and see nothing other than what is immediate, tangible and real. (This is not to say that the immediate is understood to be devoid of meaning.) A world view cannot be met or challenged by appealing to a framework of which the viewer knows nothing.

I know a Christian dance group who choreograph and perform dances on biblical themes such as the creation. The assumption is that the audience will look at their dance on creation, connect the dance with their understanding of the biblical story and then reconsider what they had previously thought of the story. The dance I saw left me challenged by the vigour, energy and joy with which Eve celebrated her being brought to life. But the implication of our youth and world view research findings is that if someone 'unchurched' watched the dance, they would not have the previous knowledge of the creation story to use as a framework necessary to interpret it. For them the dance would just be a dance – technically good or otherwise – but not a vehicle that triggered reflections on the Christian story.

I commissioned Mel Lloyd to paint a picture for a seminar room at Ridley Hall. The picture is a riot of seven different colours entitled 'Creation'. The students in training are all Christian youth and community workers, and so can use their understanding of the creation story to interpret the picture. However, if someone who had no knowledge of the biblical story saw the picture then they would not see it as a representation of the creation, but simply as a picture – nothing more, nothing less. People take out of a situation whatever they read into it. When Chelsea beat Arsenal in the quarter-finals of the European Championship in 2004, Roman Abramovich, Chelsea's billionaire Russian owner, described the team as showing Russian character to hold on, to fight and to win. On the same day, Alan Smith, the columnist in the *Daily Telegraph*, described the team as being of 'good English stock'. Their own nationalities defined their interpretation.

The idea that how we interpret something is defined by the context and purpose is crystallized within the thinking of Michael Polanyi. He illustrated this by pointing out that it would generally be considered more significant if a person were the five-thousandth visitor to a shop (because 5,000 is a round number) rather than the five thousand and thirty-second (Polanyi, 1983:33). In academic terms, this is referred to as the theory-dependence of knowledge: something is understood to be as it is because of the theoretical framework within which it has been interpreted.

Another illustration given by Polanyi was that of a stationmaster in Wales, arranging rocks to spell 'Welcome to Wales'. A week later these stones were scattered randomly by a storm. There was more significance in the stones when they were carefully arranged to spell 'Welcome to Wales' than when they were scattered randomly.

> If and only if we believe in witches may we burn people as witches; if and only if we believe in God will we build churches; if we believe in master races we may exterminate Jews and Poles; if in class war we may join the Communist party; if in guilt we may feel remorse and punish offenders; if in guilt-complexes, we may apply psychoanalysis instead; and so on. (Polanyi, 1983:113)

There are three theological objections that could be raised against the blunt prognosis that if people do not have the concepts to understand, nor the words to express, then they will not be in a position to recognize the reality of Jesus as the Saviour of the world. The first is that human beings are made in the image of God (Genesis 1.26) and that this denotes an inherent capacity for recognition of God. The argument around the idea of the image of God is that even if there is no conscious, rational recognition of the reality of God, this does not exclude the possibility of an instinctive, subconscious acknowledgement. However, there is a considerable debate over the meaning of the word 'image'. The idea that 'image' refers to a divine spark within humanity is often taken to be more Platonic than Christian in origin, since it suggests a division between the flesh and the spirit where the flesh is mistrusted and wrong and the spirit is good and of God. The alternative view is that 'image' refers to the idea that both human beings and God express their nature through mutuality and relationship.

The second possible objection is that creation itself denotes the reality of God. 'God's invisible qualities – his eternal power and divine nature – have been clearly seen, being understood from what has been made, so that men are without excuse' (Romans 1.20). God's divine nature can be seen in creation, but this does not reduce the responsibility of the Christian believer to interpret the ways of God to those outside of the faith. Equipping people with the language of recognition is not denying the external reality of God's presence in creation. To someone with a religious frame of reference, creation does portray the invisible qualities of God. To someone with a biological frame of reference, creation will portray the realities of biology. What is understood still depends on what is being looked for.

Third, it could be argued that recognition of God is dependent on the Holy Spirit (1 Corinthians 12.3) rather than on any previously held knowledge of the credal faith. The idea is that understanding is dependent on prior knowledge, and without this prior knowledge an 'unchurched' person will not automatically have the interpretative skills to acknowledge something as a Christian initiative. This does not preclude the possibility of a direct intervention of the Holy Spirit. The sovereign intervention of God will always transcend any human situation, and simply to pray and wait on God to act is a form of quietism specifically cautioned against in Thessalonians (cf. 1 Thessalonians 4.11–12), where members of the church had abandoned their day-to-day living to wait upon the Day of the Lord. Even in instances of dramatic intervention by the Holy Spirit there is still a need for a language of interpretation.

In seeking to explain the idea of God's redemptive love to someone with no concept of sin, Christians face the difficulty of trying to convey an experience that is not like any other of which that person is aware. I am a habitual marathon runner and have run more than a dozen marathons. I potter round at a steady pace that I know I can maintain, and am not really worried about improving my time or beating my personal best. The reality of being fit enough to do this is that the rhythm of running a marathon leaves me feeling mellow and relaxed. For me, running a marathon involves going into my head and running until I stop. I have tried – but completely failed – on a number of occasions to explain my marathon running experience to people for whom running for a train is a feat in itself. The idea of marathon running leaving someone feeling mellow has no resonance for them. It meets with no similar reality in their mind, and therefore it sounds ridiculous.

The assumption that there is a dormant Christian knowledge waiting to be activated is reflected within some aspects of youth and community work. There is an ethos of the youth worker needing to earn the right to talk about Christ – suspicion is assumed where it might just as easily be the case that someone will be quite willing to hear, listen and engage with the Christian story. This faulty premise lies hidden within what is known as 'relational youth work'. Its rationale is that if a young person respects the youth and community worker, then they will eventually want to understand and respond to the Christian motivation of the youth worker; this would then mean that the young person would reconsider their previously held perception of Christianity. But clearly the young person is not going to reconsider a previously held perception of Christianity if they didn't have a previously held perception of Christianity in the first place.

If the suggestion made by our youth and world view research is correct, and the 'unchurched' young person does not have the prior Christian understanding with which to interpret the character and actions of the youth worker, then a reliable person they trust will be nothing more than a reliable person they trust, and not an indicator that Christianity might be worth considering after all. A good relationship with the youth worker will not be understood by the young person as a validity-check for Christianity, since the youth worker cannot authenticate something of which the young person is not even aware. The idea that a good relationship with a youth worker might trigger young people to ask questions about the faith is largely based on wishful thinking if the young person does not have any sense of what the youth worker is hoping they will ask questions about. The youth worker cannot assume that a young person will have the knowledge base to understand and interpret what they are doing and therefore they will need to explain the Christian framework and motivation for what they do. Action might be needed to authenticate, but words are also needed to substantiate. Without this there will not be enough knowledge of a Christian world view in the young person's head to form the questions that the youth worker will be hoping they might ask.

The reality of this situation was encapsulated in a comment from Moira, a Generation Y woman in training for ordination. 'Believe me,' she said, 'if you ask a Generation Y young person what a rock is, they will tell you that it is a rock.' In the same way, a pebble thrown into the water may look pretty, but it is not going to make someone imagine their sins being washed away. Suzie, a youth worker of the same age in Luton, echoed this attitude. She was being lectured in college on the art of detached youth work. The lecturer suggested that if she sat down next to young people rather than standing when talking to them, they would see her as wanting to meet them on their level. Suzie said in response that if she sat down next to some young people they would simply think that she was sitting down next to them. In both Moira's comment and Suzie's reaction, there is no sense of making a generalized interpretation out of a specific situation.

If a rock is just a rock and not a metaphor for God, then people will need to be provided with sufficient Christian knowledge to help them to interpret their experiences and potentially to think about the Christian faith. Last Christmas, my church put on a nativity play and I was commissioned to produce a script. I went to two different Christian bookshops and could not find a straight presentation of the nativity scripted up as a play. Each version of the nativity had a twist to it; one had the shepherds singing 'There's an angel in the sky, dear shepherd' (sung to the tune of 'There's a hole in my bucket'). The assumption seemed to be that people would know the Christian story and need some new angle on it to stimulate their jaded palates. The marketing strategy did not seem to account for the fact that people might not actually know the nativity story and thus might be perfectly happy to listen to the original version.

Paul could build his presentation of the Christian message on the recognition that there was a common currency of under-standing as to what was meant by the idea of worshipping God – what they worshipped as an unknown God, he was going to make known (cf. Acts 17.23). This common currency of percep-tion and knowledge about God is largely absent for the 'unchurched' young person. What understanding they may have about God is often in the form of free-floating and sometimes col-liding pieces of information. I had a conversation with one young woman who asked me whether we were made from monkeys, God or man's left rib. She had always thought that we came from God, her friend had told her that we came from monkeys, and she had seen a church service on TV that suggested we came from man's left rib. In one sense, it would not have made any difference what answer I had given to her, because she would still lack the framework to interpret these three different theories of creation. In a context where up to 80 per cent of schools are not meeting the 1988 requirements for religious education, the responsibility for providing this framework is reverting back to the Church. The vision of Ezekiel 37 was of a valley of dry bones brought to life by the word of the Lord. The implication from our youth and world view research is that the basic skeleton of Christian knowl-edge needs to be put in place before the dry bones can be brought to life.

3

Language of Choice

The previous two chapters have established that the Church is dealing with ignorance rather than hostility or apathy in relation to the Christian message. In this, the last of the scene-setting chapters, I propose that this is not, however, a straightforward problem–solution situation: people may know very little about the Christian faith, but it is not the case that they can simply be told. The reason is all to do with language. Underpinning the contemporary use of language is an assumption of choice and personal preference. If I make a claim about Jesus Christ, I am heard as making a statement of choice rather than a truth claim. This means that talking about faith is inevitably characterized by ambiguity simply because, initially, I am likely to be misunderstood.

People like to talk about themselves, and attach a lot of significance to their experiences. People rely on their own experiences more than on the direction and inspiration of others in how they live their lives. A survey in the *Sun* (8 September 2003) reported that inspiring figures such as Christ, Princess Diana or Nelson Mandela were not the biggest influence on how people lived their lives. The biggest influence of all was the conclusions people drew from their own experiences of life (cited by 62 per cent). It sometimes appears that the ultimate justification of any choice is the comment: 'It felt right to me.'

Language Shapes Behaviour

Language affects people's self-perception. It is both imitative and constitutive in that it both expresses or describes (imitates) and creates (constitutes) ideas and feelings. Language is imitative in the sense that it describes an external reality. There is an agreed set of social understandings as to what is meant by specific objects such as 'tree', 'spade' or 'garden'. These objects are being described rather than created by the words. Sometimes words seem inadequate for the task set before them, but loving someone, for example, is still loving someone, however poor the language of description. Language is also constitutive in the sense that when I articulate a sentiment, I do (to an extent) experience that sentiment. If I use the phrase 'I love you' to someone else, I am using the words both to describe how things are and also how I would like things to be. It is through language that I describe the actual person I see myself to be and the ideal person that I would like to become. Once something is said then it takes on a life of its own. This is true for the positive language of love and the negative language of anger; things are better, or worse, once they are voiced. If, for example, I say that I am angry, then I have given life to the situation. It was with good reason that in my family there were clear 'Christmas rules', including: if you have not got anything nice to say then you should not say anything at all.

Language feeds imagination and self-understanding. I dislike the habit of asking for a 'quick' word; I feel that if I am constantly talking of doing something in haste, then I might be internalizing a sense of pressure and obligation. By contrast, Michael Caine described people who spoke slowly as people who expected to be listened to. Language normalizes a behaviour pattern or way of relating to the world. Kathleen McGowan (*Independent*, 20 January 2004) listed different impulses that, in her opinion, have become normal patterns of behaviour. Her list includes:

- 'emotional rubbernecking' – an interest in tragedy, as exemplified in the way people might boast about 'near misses';
- 'adultery fantasy' – the idea that sexual fantasy will not lead to betrayal and is to be encouraged;
- 'money matters' – accepting the reality of people being status conscious;
- 'grief relief' – the reality of mixed motives when someone dies after a long and difficult illness.

What is common to each impulse described is that they are not setting out an ideal view of how human behaviour could be, but a pragmatic view of how human behaviour actually is. But what happens is that, being encapsulated in these neat descriptions, these behaviours acquire a validity they did not necessarily have previously, and thus move towards becoming accepted norms rather than occasional extremes. This is because, once something is articulated, it becomes more standardized.

The notion of language affecting behaviour and offering an insight into human nature is nothing new. Bragg (2003:146) draws attention to the fact that well over 2,000 of our words are first recorded by Shakespeare. The extent of his creative power with words is indicated by the vocabulary of his work, which is reckoned to be at least 21,000 words (the King James Bible, published in 1611, used only about 10,000 different words). And it is not only individual words; many phrases have passed into the idiom of the English language. Bragg cites just a few from *Hamlet*: 'cruel only to be kind', 'in my mind's eye', 'though this be madness yet there is method in it', and 'more in sorrow than in anger'.

I saw a working demonstration of the ability of Shakespeare's language to influence self-perception in a local primary school production, in Cambridge, of *A Midsummer Night's Dream*. The director of the play was RADA tutor Helen Strange. She began by telling the story, and letting the children act out different scenes using their own words. She set up various scenes for the children, which paralleled scenes from the play. She focused on certain themes: relationships between friends and family, power over others, the use of magic, how to put on a play, melodrama and celebration. After beginning with free improvisation, the work became more structured as Shakespeare's actual lines were fed into the rehearsals in the form of suggestions over how the scenes might be understood. The children were allowed to speak either in their own words or in Shakespeare's. Some found the language very exciting and wanted more; some preferred to use their own language until they felt more comfortable with the situation they were given. Ultimately every child became curious about the Shakespearean language and enjoyed speaking it. Rather than the words being a barrier to understanding, they became essential to the young people being able to understand the characters' actions and intentions more fully. What began as unnatural modes of speech became the norm and it was the modern parlance that became awkward. Even if the words were not always fully understood, the language was shaping how the young people understood the different scenes of the play.

The same idea was demonstrated by a project performing plays of Shakespeare in Broadmoor (Cox, 1992). This experiment in psychology set out to see if Shakespeare could be used to reflect back to the patients their insights into themselves and, for some, the true nature of their acts of violence.

> He told me how some of his patients had written about Macbeth for an 'O' or 'A' level exam. In a discussion a patient said, 'When I killed someone, it wasn't like that', or 'it was exactly like that'. (Rylance, 1992:27)

Shakespeare provided opportunities for self-knowledge and for the patients to work out things about themselves they would never have been able to do on their own. The purpose of playing 'was and is, to hold, as 'twere, the mirror up to nature' (*Hamlet* iii.2.20).

A mirror is something that faithfully reflects or gives a true picture of something else; something worth imitating – the *ad~mire?*

French and Latin root of a mirror is both to 'look at' and 'wonder'. (Cox, 1992:5)

The Shaping Effect of Bible Language

Just as it is with Shakespeare, so also it is with the Bible. The language of the Bible has provided a mirror of how people have understood themselves and how they have interpreted their place in the world. The Christian discourse is not just about people understanding God, but is also about people understanding themselves. The language of the Bible does not simply provide people with a set of beliefs, but also offers ideas, images and stories about how they might interpret and live out their lives. The Bible is full of insights into human nature that are applicable to a person, whether or not they call themselves a Christian.

When Jesus talked about turning the other cheek (Matthew 5.39), he did not mean that you should give up and give in, but rather that you shouldn't hit back and score points. If someone is angry with you and you get angry in return, then the issue the other person has to deal with is your anger. If someone gets angry with you and you do not get angry in return, then the issue that remains is the other person's anger – which they have to deal with. 'Turn the other cheek', therefore, is not simply a command about how to behave, but also an insight into a potentially confrontational situation. Put simply, if you hit back, you will escalate the situation and make it a lot worse!

Similarly, the idea of taking 'an eye for an eye' (Deuteronomy 19.21) was not a call for vengeance, but a directive on proportionate response. In other words, it meant do not take *more* than an eye for an eye; not, as is sometimes assumed, that you have the right to take *at least* an eye for an eye. This idea of proportionate response has been a key principle underlying the theory of a 'just war' and is a basis of the philosophical thinking upon which the legitimacy of armed conflict is still assessed. The idea of responsibility is enshrined in the image of being 'my brother's keeper' (Genesis 4.9) and not 'passing by on the other side' (Luke 10.32). Rights and responsibilities are the two great, conflicting ideals that animate all political debate: our rights as individuals and our responsibilities as members of society.

There are many key Christian concepts that together offer insight into behaviour patterns while avoiding a straight two-dimensional morality. The idea of not storing up 'treasures on earth' (Matthew 6.19) tells you not to live for tomorrow. The idea of a 'thorn in my flesh' (2 Corinthians 12.7) tells you that not everything works out. The idea of being as 'shrewd as snakes and innocent as doves' (Matthew 10.16) tells you to be discerning and careful. The Beatitudes (Matthew 5) tell you that happiness is best defined by a sense of inner peace. The Bible offers clear paradigms of how to understand and relate to the world. Love, for example, is presented as a total concern for the well-being of another (1 Corinthians 13). This is a concept that can liberate and legitimate people's ideal aspirations of themselves.

Even the negative emotions expressed in the Bible can offer you comfort in reflecting your own thoughts and feelings back to you. There can be a sense of relief for soneone in seeing some of the darker side of life dealt with in a story. A contemporary example of this is the current popularity of Jacqueline Wilson's novels, which are currently the most borrowed books in public libraries – above the likes of Catherine Cookson and J. K. Rowling. Her books portray experiences such as divorce, parental failing, illness and death. Everything works out in the end, but the suspense is maintained throughout the book. In the same way the psalms provide a language for negative feelings. You might never want to dash an infant's head against the rocks (Psalm 137.9) but there is a comfort in knowing that the psalmist was angry enough to want to do so. In the New Testament as well, stories give voice to negative emotions. Peter and Paul met only three times and each time had a row, mostly about whether to allow the Gentiles into the church (e.g. Acts 15). In Galatians Paul is so angry that he suggests that those who support circumcision for new converts should go the whole hog and emasculate themselves (Galatians 5.12). The disciples argued about who among them was the greatest (Mark 9.34).

Barriers to Understanding

There are, however, two significant factors that hinder the continuing contribution of biblical images, stories and poetry to the public awareness and imagination. The first is a lack of basic understanding about Christianity in the public domain, as described in the previous chapters. When religious imagery is used it is generally removed from anything of its original context. Dot Cotton walking around in *EastEnders* quoting Scripture: 'Greater love hath no man than this, that a man lay down his life for his friend' (John 15.13 AV) (episode on 17 February 2004) appeared absurd because it was decontextualized. In the *News of the World* (24 January 2004), Abi Titmuss was described as a 'fallen angel' over the story that she was recorded by her then boyfriend John Leslie having sex with other men, women and himself. 'It's our fun tape taken over a long period of time.'

The idea of God and heaven is also frequently parodied and caricatured in popular culture. In a television advert for Philadelphia cheese, an angel is pictured doing yoga as a way of coping with her 24/7 lifestyle. In another television advert for Walkers' crisps, ex-England soccer manager, Terry Venables, played the devil. Dressed all in red, with horns on his head, 'El Tel' appeared urging Gary Lineker to steal crisps from a child. Fellow ex-England boss Bobby Robson played a winged angel all in white, telling his former captain Gary to be good. More extreme is the musical show *Jerry Springer – The Opera*, where Jerry Springer hosts his show in hell with the devil demanding an apology from Jesus. Jesus is told to 'get over' the crucifixion because it happened 2,000 years ago and the devil is told by Jesus holding up his hand to 'talk to the stigmata'. The action culminates in Jesus and the devil dancing about the stage, swearing at each other in operatic tones. When I expressed an unease at the end of the show, I was told by the ushers not to worry because it was nothing more than a 'silly show designed to make money'. There was absolutely no sense of the play being seen as a part of an exchange of ideas about the Christian faith. In fact it passed off as nothing more significant than a Saturday night entertainment for those who could afford £50 seats.

The second factor hindering the contribution of biblical images, stories, poetry and ideas to public awareness is that people are out of practice in talking about God and that consequently language has lost the capacity to express religious ideas. Whatever the subject under discussion, I need to use words that people will understand. To acquire and express definite meaning, language must be poor enough to allow the same words to be used a sufficient number of times (Polanyi, 1983:78); there has to be a shared understanding of what the words mean.

For many people in Britain, God is seen as an optional extra rather than an underpinning reality in life. This viewpoint is a logical consequence of the way language has developed into different ways of expressing choice. Macintyre (1990:10–11) suggests that within contemporary use of language any apparent assertion of principles is actually just a mask for expressions of personal preference. 'Emotivism' is the doctrine that all evaluative judgements are nothing but expressions of preference, expressions of attitude or feeling insofar as they are moral or evaluative in character. This results in a lack of language adequate to talk about God.

If it is accepted that language is an expression of preference and choice then it can be recognized that people's understanding of God will be interpreted in this way too. This is because the conclusions that people draw come out of the information that they start with. My father, who was a lawyer, illustrated this. He explained to me that when confronted by an opposing piece of legal advice, he would ask to see the information upon which the advice had been given. In this way he was able to discern the basis on which a decision had been made. His point was that it was the interpretation of this information that would shape the advice given by the lawyer. It was pointless challenging the advice on its own, since the advice might be a reasonable set of conclusions to draw from the original information. The advice was shaped by the original information; therefore it was this, rather than the advice itself, that should be challenged.

The Influence of a Choice Culture

Choice is all-important in how language is formed and, since language affects people's self-perception, choice is equally important in how ideas are shaped. In the *Matrix* film, *Revolutions*, Agent Smith (Hugo Weaving) was locked in a ferocious climactic battle with Neo (Keanu Reeves). They clashed endlessly on land and in the air with neither one seeming to take any real damage. Finally, the two knocked each other to the ground. There seemed to be no way around it. The two were equal. Agent Smith tried to discourage Neo, attacking his humanity. He proceeded to demean all the emotions and experiences that humankind held dear. His final attack was something along the lines of: all of those things you hold dear are just simple constructs of the fallible human mind in a pitiful effort to justify your own existence. So why do you continue to fight when it's all so meaningless? What did Neo reply? Did he justify his humanity by simply saying that Agent Smith was wrong or that he could never understand how real those things were to the people who believe in them? No, he used as a justification the idea that he fought because he could fight. 'I fight because I choose to. Because I can, I choose to fight.' So Neo simply did something because he could, because choosing is seen here as the most human and valid thing a being can do.

This same idea occurs in the final part of *Harry Potter and the Chamber of Secrets*. The book had turned on the question 'who is the heir of Slytherin?' That was to say, who was the inheritor of evil? Harry had noticed many similarities between himself and the evil wizard he had been fighting. He wondered if the sorting hat, which had chosen him for Gryffindor, the school house to which he belonged, had made the wrong choice and that he should have been in Slytherin house. Dumbledore, the head-master, acknowledges the likeness he fears, but then points to (what he saw as) the significance of choices.

> 'Voldemort put a bit of himself in *me*?,' Harry said, thunder-struck.
>
> 'It certainly seems so.'
>
> 'So I *should* be in Slytherin,' said Harry, looking desperately in Dumbledore's face . . . 'It only put me in Gryffindor,' said Harry in a defeated voice, 'because I asked not to go in Slytherin . . .'
>
> '*Exactly*,' said Dumbledore, beaming once more. 'Which makes you very *different* . . . it is our choices, Harry, that show us what we truly are.' (Rowling, 1998: 245)

Reflections on the importance of choice are not a new theme for literature. In Book I (Lines 1–263) of Milton's *Paradise Lost*, Satan and his lieutenant discuss their options and choices, having just lost the war against God. In *Paradise Lost*, though, the discussion about choice takes place within a clear theological world view. In the *Matrix* and *Harry Potter*, the validity of choice is assumed to be self-defining – the point is making the choice, not what the choice actually is. If every choice is as good as every other choice, then there is no option with any special value. In this situation, traditional exaltations of the specialness of Christianity fall flat on their face. I might want to say, 'This really is the way, you know', but people will inevitably be hear-ing, 'It's just another way.' It is like having 1,000 TV channels; where do people start? If they are all as good as each other, is there a point in watching any of them?

There is such a thing as too much choice. Schwartz (2004)

wrote that once a society's level of per-capita wealth crosses a threshold from poverty to adequate subsistence, further increases in national wealth have almost no effect on happiness. I lived in India for two years and found that there was less self-pity among the people I met than I would find among a comparable group of people in England. I reckon to meet two or three people in England each week with some form of 'chip on their shoulder' from some unreconciled conflict or some unfulfilled expectations. In India, I met two or three such people in two years. I returned from my two years abroad thinking that self-pity could be the luxury of choice.

A choice – such as that made by one young person on a weekend residential course when he said, 'I want chips with salt and I want them now!' – is not necessarily a good thing. Schwartz (2004) talked about the tyranny of small choices and wrote that people would be better off if they embraced certain voluntary constraints on their freedom of choice. On a trip to the cinema I was told that vanilla ice cream was not available and I had to choose between maple, pecan, pistachio, chocolate chip cookie . . . and several other exotic flavours. It did not, in fact, enhance my evening's enjoyment, since I was required to give energy and 'head space' to something for which I had no inclination. Schwartz quotes an experiment where people were offered the chance to taste different varieties of jam that were available for sale. In one condition, people were offered a choice of six varieties for tasting; in another 24 varieties were available.

In either case, the entire set of 24 varieties was available for purchase. The large array of jams attracted more people to the table than the small array, though in both cases people tasted the same number of jams on average. When it came to buying, however, a huge difference became evident. Thirty per cent of the people exposed to the small array of jams actually bought a jar; only 3 per cent of those exposed to the large array of jams did so. (Schwartz, 2004:19–20)

If there is one building above any other that exemplifies the importance given to choice it is the supermarket. The supermarket, and not the church, is the building in the community where people of all ages might congregate at some stage during the week. Supermarket buildings can appear with tall clock towers in mock religious splendour. People can go to the supermarket to take out insurance, book a holiday, buy medicine, clothes, music, furniture – and still have time to buy the groceries for that evening. Tesco have introduced the 'trim trolley' that can be set to different levels of resistance, making it harder or easier to push. This is designed to make a typical 40-minute supermarket shop into the equivalent of a gentle workout. In September 2001, Joanne Hamlyn and Charlie Hefferman were the first couple to have a supermarket wedding (at Asda superstore in Elgin, Scotland), and it is even possible to register a birth in a supermarket. The idea of multiple choice is ingrained within the ethos of supermarket shopping.

Ingrained assumptions about the value of choice also appear through the ethos of business. In business terms, it is second nature for people to talk about there 'being a market' for an idea or to 'buy into' a situation. Consumerism – which embodies the choice culture – frames the discussion about people in terms of series of choices. This can lead to a mechanical view of personhood. The language is easily absorbed: if you split up you are described as 'decoupling'; if you are seen as no longer contributing to the firm's output you are 'dead wood'; if you want to spend more time with your family you are seen as 'downsizing'; if you are successful in making money you are seen as 'making a killing'; if you are laid off, you have got 'bounced'; and if you make the wrong choice, then you may find you have made a CLM – a 'career-limiting move' – that adversely affects your future.

Ingrained assumptions about the value of choice also appear through the ethos of self-help. In self-help literature you are taking control of how you perceive yourself and how you act. This is empowering you to choose. Obstacles to choice are to be

overcome. For example, fear can be seen as an obstacle to realizing choice, so Jeffers (1997) suggests: 'Feel the fear and do it
anyway' – expressing the view that the only way to get rid of a
fear of something is to go out and do it. She suggests repeating
out loud the phrase, 'I am powerful and I am loved' at least 25
times every morning, noon and night. Gray (2002) writes that
fear is instilled in us by over-anxious parents, pointing out that
it is a rare mother who calls out to their child as they go off to
school, 'Take a lot of risks today, darling!' Gray also encourages
people to believe in their inner genius and to write a love letter
to 'the child within' at least once a week.

It is because the ethos of personal choice has so thoroughly
seeped into the use of language that there are often no words
equal to the task of talking about the fact of God. Newbiggin
(1989) wrote that the Church exists as witness to certain beliefs
about what is the case – about facts not values. If I make the
statement that Jesus Christ is the Son of God, I may want to say
it as a statement of fact but it is more likely to be heard as a matter of opinion. The original meaning of the word is that of the
Latin *factum*, 'something which has been done, or accom-
plished'. A fact is something that has happened. In the original
sense, one may properly say that the gospel is a statement of
facts, of what God has done. But in contemporary society the
gospel is heard by people as being about opinions rather than
facts. The language available to me allows me space only to
describe the gospel through the terminology of values and opinions. Hence my talking about the gospel is only ever heard as
being a result of my choice rather than God's revelation. The
non-confessional, information-based approach to religious education has also reinforced the sense of individual choice rather
than any theological truth claim being the underpinning to any
belief structure.

Words, as stated previously, depend on a context for their
meaning and are defined by the company they keep. If someone
is preaching in a Sunday church service and they use the words
'Jesus Christ' then they will be understood in one way. If later on

the same person is driving home, a car cuts them up and they use the same words 'Jesus Christ', then they will be understood in a completely different way. In the first instance the words would have been describing the Saviour of the world and in the second instance the person would have been using words to express anger at someone else's actions.

When I evangelize, in my perception I am telling someone about the good news of Jesus Christ who lived, died and rose again. In the perception of the person listening I am telling them about an opinion that I happen to hold. To a Christian, speaking the phrase 'Jesus Christ is Lord and Saviour' is a statement of fact; it is the way that the world is. To a non-Christian, listening to the phrase 'Jesus Christ is Lord and Saviour' is simply opinion. It is nothing more than how the other person might make sense of the world and choose to live their life – I think that breakfast is the most important meal of the day; I think that light blue is a nice colour for a bedroom to be painted; and I think that Jesus Christ is my Lord and Saviour.

The Shocking Truth

If the gospel is only ever heard as choice then it can only ever be understood as something to do with feelings or actions. The gospel becomes something that is just helpful, offering people some kind of personal comfort – 'It helps me in my personal life'. Alternatively, the gospel degenerates into mere moralism – 'This is what you ought to do'. In either case it does not challenge people's understanding of the real world within which they have to live.

I met a girl, Kate, at a dinner party and she asked if I could come and bless her house. We arranged a time and I went over and did a personalized communion service. Only after I had finished did I discover that two weeks previously she had asked a spiritualist in; the week before she had invited a feng shui specialist; and I was third in line as a Christian priest. I said to her that it was rather like washing your clothes with Ajax and Daz. She replied that it was more like washing with Ajax and fabric conditioner. For Kate, Christianity was just one of several, equally attractive options available:

> Even though it still has a privileged position, Christianity is often seen as one religious option among many, which is intrinsically neither better nor truer than any of the other options, among which must be included both atheism and agnosticism. (Montefiore, 1992:3)

The idea that the gospel isn't just morality or comfort but truth is startling, even shocking to someone without the framework of language to understand it. In this respect there is an inevitable *ambiguity* in evangelism. If no language is adequate to the task of talking about God, ideas are going to be misunderstood before they are understood. Conversations about forgiveness, redemption and love are going to startle people if they are out of the context of most of their thought patterns.

To appreciate the effect of introducing a concept to someone who has not previously heard it articulated, consider what happens in the telling of a joke. I particularly like the joke about the two ducks. One duck says, 'Quack, quack.' The other duck says, 'I knew that you were going to say that.' Jokes are about wordplay, and they work because they break the expected sequence of ideas. The humour comes from exploiting our expectations – we expect one thing and get another. A dog goes in to send a telegram and writes, 'Woof, woof, woof, woof.' He is told that he can have one more word for the same price. The dog replies: 'I can't do that, it wouldn't make sense.' If Christianity is to jump out of the 'choice' box into which language has put it, then it will take people by surprise – just like a joke might.

It can be quite shocking when something unexpected and out of context is introduced. I lived in Chennai in South India for two years. A regular sight were the people collecting rubbish from the streets to sell on for a small sum. They were a striking sight: bent over, wizened old men with large sacks of rubbish perched precariously on their backs. On one occasion I was in a church for a New Year service. As the clock ticked towards midnight, one of the rubbish collectors came into the church and walked up towards the altar. He put his bag of rubbish down and looked round at everyone in the church. There was a collective intake of breath as people continued singing uneasily. People wondered whether he was mad and were nervous that he might do something dangerous or unexpected. Instead he turned back towards the altar and in a loud voice offered a prayer of thanks to God for his blessings over the previous year. He then picked up his bag and walked out of the church in the same way he had come in.

This is the first strand of ambiguity within evangelism. If it is recognized that the Christian gospel does not feature on people's landscape, then it will initially take people by surprise. Introducing an idea, though, creates it as a possibility. If I explain the idea of forgiveness then I am giving a potentially different option for someone to consider. Forgiveness offers the idea of not holding a grudge. Love offers the idea of seeking the good of another person. Redemption offers the idea of giving someone a second chance.

4

The Principles of Ambiguous Evangelism

For a period, I was student and chaplain at London South Bank University. I played rugby for the University First Fifteen. Games would be played on Wednesdays and after the game everyone would congregate at the student union bar. They were long, fun evenings, often loud and good-humoured. Late into one evening a couple had a blazing row, which finished with the boyfriend walking out, leaving his girlfriend in tears. I went to talk with her to see if she was all right but was unable to offer any real assistance because she had no sense that I was the chaplain. If I had sat in my room during office hours I would have been distinctive but not accessible enough. In the bar at 11.30 p.m. I was accessible but not distinctive enough.

This balance between distinctiveness and accessibility mirrors the nature of belief, which is a balance between knowing and not knowing (cf. Lord, I believe; help thou mine unbelief (Mark 9.24, AV). What I know of God is what he has revealed; what I do not know of God is the mystery (cf. Isaiah 6.3). Christian thinking tends to emphasize either one or the other. The first approach to theology lays emphasis on making this mystery clear and communicable to people; the second approach to theology lays emphasis on recognizing the mystery and unknowable nature of God. An emphasis on revelation will stress contextual thinking, immediacy, relevance and applicability of the gospel message; an emphasis on mystery will accentuate tradition, continuity, obedience, reverence and sacrament. If there is too much emphasis on accessibility, then Christianity can be absorbed into one particular subcultural way of doing things. If there is too much emphasis on mystery, then Christianity can end up seeming to be out of touch and irrelevant.

One of the issues at the centre of this dichotomy is the limitation of language, as referred to in the earlier discussion on the language of choice. When I am asked to preach in a church, I never feel nervous beforehand but will often feel quite shaken afterwards. These post-sermon nerves arise from a sense of disconnection at having used temporal words to describe eternal truths. It is by its very nature an impossible task. Language, by definition, is limited in what it can achieve. Polanyi (1983) talked about how one cannot say clearly how to ride a bike nor how to recognize your mackintosh; how to recognize a friend nor how to describe a face. Language that cannot describe the immediate and the functional is not going to be able to explain the mysterious and the divine. The allure of mystery, though, can leave people wanting to know more. As the prayer goes, 'What I do not know, teach me; what I may not have, give me; what I am not yet, make me, for thy holy name's sake.'

There will always be a space between the clarity of any description of God and the reality of his mystery. It is the integrity of this space that ensures people's ability to respond out of their own free volition. There is an inherent ambiguity built into a belief structure that wants people to respond out of faith and freedom of choice. Dostoevsky (1958) wrote a story about a Grand Inquisitor who had to deal with the situation of Jesus coming back to earth. The Grand Inquisitor put Jesus in prison but then visited him to explain why he needed to do this. His opinion was that Jesus made three mistakes during his temptation in the desert. The first mistake was that in deciding not to turn the stones into bread he refused to do a miracle (Matthew 4.4). The second mistake was that in refusing to throw himself down from the highest point of the Temple he refused to create a mystery out of his identity as the Messiah (Matthew 4.7). The third mistake was that in refusing the kingdoms of the earth he was careful not to allow himself to be seen as a man of authority (Matthew 4.10). The Grand Inquisitor explained to Jesus that miracle, mystery and authority are the three things that people need to feel confident in making a decision about God. Jesus' desire for people to make a decision based solely on free will meant that 'instead of firm foundations for appeasing man's conscience you chose everything that was exceptional, enigmatic and vague' (Dostoevsky, 1958:286). The Church, explained the Grand Inquisitor, had corrected Jesus' great work and based the Christian faith on miracle, mystery and authority. It is for this reason that Jesus needed to be kept in prison because if he was let out then he would make the same mistakes all over again.

What the story is highlighting is the idea that God is never meant to be fully understood. In Job 33, Job is castigated for his presumption in thinking that he could know the ways of God. If God could be perfectly comprehended then he would not be God – the divine DNA is, by definition, too big to be grasped. The essence of mystery is that it is opaque and cannot be fully understood. God is a mystery to be enjoyed, not a problem to be solved (Begbie, 2004). The role of theology is to give glory to God – to excite imagination, wonder and praise in myself and others.

There is an important distinction, though, between mystery and uncertainty, and the incarnation of Christ is the way in which God draws people into this gap between the poverty of the words available for use about God and the richness of the subject matter. Christian theology is, by definition, Christology, but people cannot be made aware of the claims of Christ until they have recognized in the first place that there is a person of Christ, who has a claim on their lives.

If it is accepted that people have only a cursory understanding of Christianity, then it can be acknowledged that a clear and recognizable Church is not going to put people off because there is no prejudgement in their response. If anything, some of the success enjoyed by the Orthodox Church, Catholicism and strict evangelicalism, for example, is a result of people being drawn by something clearly defined to which they can belong. People cannot be talked, argued or cajoled, tempted, lured or enticed into the kingdom of heaven. Making a story contemporary does not make it relevant. *Romeo and Juliet* acted in modern costume still presents the identical themes of love and rivalry. Similarly a Church designed to be culturally relevant still presents the same challenging gospel message.

It is the suggestion of *Ambiguous Evangelism* that the claims of Christ can best be presented playfully, through story, in an understated manner, and through dialogue. The claims of Christ can be presented:

- playfully because appealing to someone's imagination can be stronger than appealing to their intellect – initially, people will generally respond more to passion and feeling than to clarity and understanding.
- through story because the narrative forms an easy way for people to appropriate ideas and thoughts into their own context.
- in an understated manner, where appropriate, in order to encourage people to come back and ask questions.
- through encouraging a dialogue and exchange of ideas with the other person, because belief is not a subject that can be dealt with in one single conversation or presentation.

Talking about the Human Figure of Jesus will Provoke a Response

The word 'challenge' has gathered rather aggressive connotations, but it is in fact a gentler word than modern usage tends to imply. It means literally 'to lay claim to'. Talking about the person of Jesus challenges people. The disciples knew Jesus as a man before they knew him as God. Talking to people first about the human Jesus rather than the divine God recreates this pattern of discovery and learning. It starts with recognizable human emotion and activity and moves towards the more abstract spiritual idea of God. Jesus was hungry (Matthew 4.2), thirsty (John 19.28) and weary (John 4.6). He wept (John 11.35), sighed (Mark 7.34), groaned (Mark 8.12) and glared (Mark 3.5). He was agitated (John 11.33), angry (Mark 3.5) and annoyed (Mark 10.14). He was both joyful (Luke 10.21) and desolate (Matthew 27.46). Looking at the Gospels before the Epistles mirrors the process of God's revelation, since the Epistles were written as a response to the Gospels.

The popularity of 'What would Jesus do?' (WWJD) badges points to the appeal of asking a tangible and immediate question when inviting people to think about God. 'What would Jesus do?' is an open question, and 'Do you know that God loves you?' is a closed question. The question about God's love is abstract and conceptual. It puts the person being questioned into an entirely passive role. The question about Jesus Christ is tangible and immediate. It requires a response and it puts the person being questioned into an active role. In presenting challenges, open questions are more effective than closed ones. An open question is one that asks someone to express an opinion in response. A closed question is one that can be answered with a simple 'yes' or 'no'. 'Do you like this suit?' is therefore a closed question and 'What do you think of this suit?' is an open question.

The idea of the Son of God being crucified and then rising from the dead fits no world view but its own and therefore it obliges people to respond. As discussed previously, people take out of something what they read into it. In the case of the cross, they are either given life or condemned by their response. Paul talked about preaching Christ crucified; he said it was 'a stumbling-block to Jews and foolishness to Gentiles, but to those whom God has called, both Jews and Greeks, Christ the power of God and the wisdom of God' (1 Corinthians 1.23–24). He was recognizing the need to run the risk of putting people off. It is only those who are determined to find out the truth who will succeed in doing so. A key part of having the cross as the central symbol of faith is that

74

(initially) it is hard to understand (place), and in being so it requires people to work at what it means.

In October 2003 the American illusionist David Blane chose to spend 44 days without food, suspended in a glass box next to Tower Bridge in London. The event received a lot of publicity and over the period provoked dislike and admiration in equal measures. Sylvie, who came with me to see the sight, was startled at the strength of her reaction. She had thought that she would simply be interested. However, when she arrived, she looked at young teenage women screaming in pop-idol-type delight at a man choosing to starve himself while suspended 20 feet in the air and thought the whole thing macabre and distasteful. Such was the baseness of the idea of a man deliberately starving himself simply for the challenge, publicity and money he would receive, that she felt unable to maintain her characteristic detached interest and was instead forced into the more basic response of distaste.

The point of maximizing publicity for a deliberate exercise in self-starvation was simply to get a reaction; there was no attempt to put forward a point of view to the people watching. People reacted instinctively and often aggressively. There were eggs and golf balls thrown at the glass box. If people did not like it, then they would, at the least, be talking about it. There was a magnetic quality to the exercise in that it either attracted or repelled people. Neutrality was not an option – you either loved it or you hated it. The crucifixion, for Paul, had this same stark quality about it in that it provoked a response in the people listening to his preaching (1 Cor. 1.23). There is an extent to which if someone is not shocked by the cross then they have not understood it.

The Use of Play

Plato said that you can discover more about a person in an hour of play than in a year of conversation. Malbon (1999:12) suggested that the notion of play is under-acknowledged as a framework for interpreting people's identity. He talked of playful vitality as a way of understanding people, in that it is only in their play that people can choose what they want to do and therefore it is in play that what is important to people can be recognized. Fun, play and creativity are not optional extras but key virtues in someone exploring and understanding their identity and place in the world.

People can be more open to new ideas if they are made to laugh rather than frown. A lawyer friend told me the story of an occasion when, as a barrister in court, she attended a newly divorced couple discussing the custody arrangements for their child. The insults between the couple were so strong that she and the clerk of the courts were initially shocked but then amazed. Each time one of the two said something, the other would cap it with a stronger retort. My barrister friend and the clerk caught each other's eyes and, to her horror, they started to giggle and then to laugh. For a few seconds the couple were angry at this intrusion, but then they also laughed at the absurdity of their insults towards each other. Once they had all laughed together, a settlement over the needs of the child was then quickly agreed.

I have found that people generally respond better to praise than to criticism. Paul starts the letter to the Philippians by praising the church. I have a self-made compliment rule that I will always pass on a favourable comment that one person has made about another. When I am marking a student's essay, I will put first what has been done well followed only then by what could be improved. 'People like unexpected praise', I was told by a colleague. 'Tell me that I am an intelligent woman,' she said, 'and it will not mean a lot because I already know that I am intelligent. Tell me that I am beautiful, then it will be more unexpected and I will be pleased and taken by surprise.' Say to a comedian they are funny and they glaze over because they get laughs on stage every night. Tell them they are sensitive to the human condition and they will be pleased you have seen something many do not.

What this means in terms of evangelism is that priority needs to be given to acknowledging what someone has got right ahead of criticizing what they have got wrong. Truth has its own self-justification – adultery is wrong because marriage is right. Drunkenness can be criticized because self-control is a virtue. Cruelty is to be condemned because gentleness is to be commended. People need something positive to hold onto – not just to be made aware of negatives. When someone is climbing they will not let go of one piece of rope before they have secured themselves to another. People are creatures of habit and need to take on an idea before they let an old idea go; they need a good alternative to a bad resident thought. It is similar to telling a smoker to quit smoking. They are more likely to succeed if they have something they can move on to, such as chewing gum or whistling, than if they are just left to concentrate on the thing they have to change. It is only reasonable to suggest ways to move forward, to present ideas to replace other ones.

This can be done through appealing to people's imagination. Imagination is integral to the idea of play. Cat, a lay pastor, related to me an idea she had heard: that school assemblies are 'flirting, not flashing' – they are showing people something but leaving them wanting more. People can be open to new ideas if what they are hearing someone appeal to their imagination. To play is to take a make-believe situation as real – 'Imagine that you are in prison and I am going to set you free,' one child says to another. To play is to take a self-contained situation as being total – in football, the game is treated as all-important for the 90 minutes of the match; in a game of cards, a set of rules is self-referencing.

A group of us made a game out of planning a feast along with a collection of different young people. People gave us money and we received a grant from a trust. We ended up with £200 to spend on a meal that would be held in church and would act out the parable of the banquet (Matthew 22.1–14).

We spent it on turkey and chicken and ham and crisps. To start with we did not know whether we would have enough food but we ended with enough for one hundred and fifty people to walk out of the church with their bellies full . . . when we took a group out to do some shopping for the feast they could not believe they had so much money to spend and that they could buy whatever they wanted. They kept on wanting to steal things and I kept on telling them there was no need and that we could buy it. The trip to the supermarket was an acted out parable of the love of God. If the young people could not understand that if they wanted a bar of white chocolate they could have it by right and not steal it, then what chance did they have of working out that eternal life was theirs by right? (Mayo, 1996:99)

On one occasion I started a talk in a church by offering 50p pieces to anyone in the congregation who was prepared publicly to ask for one. People were hesitant to ask for a variety of reasons: it was an unexpected thing to be asked to do in the context of a sermon; nobody wanted to be the first; people were not sure what other people might think of them, were they to say that they would like the 50p. I then made my point in drawing a parallel between asking for a 50p in church and asking God for the free gift of eternal life (Luke 11.9). The rationale was that if people did not trust me enough to accept my offer of 50p then how were they going to trust God enough to accept his offer of eternal life?

parables In the early stages of a conversation it can be more powerful to appeal to people's imagination than to their emotion or intellect since feelings precede thinking and interest precedes understanding. Our youth and world view research (see Chapter 3) was conducted through group interviews with young people. I would show the group an image or play them a piece of music and ask for their response. As directed by Sara, if I asked the question, 'What do you *think* of that?' I would get an answer that was cognitive and conceptual. If I asked the question 'What do you *feel* about that?' I would get two answers for the price of one: the interviewees' answers would be affective and emotive as well as potentially cognitive and conceptual.

'Intellectual passions affirm the scientific interest and value of certain facts as against a lack of interest and value in others. The scientist has to care; originality needs to be passionate' (Polanyi, 1983:159). Christian truth can be appreciated intuitively before it is understood conceptually. Polanyi understood beauty as a clue to significance. 'We cannot truly account for our acceptance of such theories without endorsing our acknowledgement of a beauty that exhilarates and a profundity that entrances us' (Polanyi, 1983:15).

The Use of Story

After the release of *Schindler's List*, my cousin David said to me that it was not the role of Hollywood to teach us about the Holocaust. My response to this comment was, 'Why not?' Narrative is an easy, accessible and user-friendly method of communicating information or truth, and stories always appeal to people's imagination. Mel Gibson's film *The Passion of the Christ* has been both strongly admired and attacked. The phenomenon of the film's success, though, is an indication of the effectiveness of an unashamedly told powerful story. Stories feed people's imagination. During 2001–2003, our youth and world view research team monitored the *EastEnders* website message boards. The message board for storyline always had far more entries (sometimes up to ten times more) than the boards for either character or issue.

The argument in favour of using stories to communicate Christian truth is compelling. Over 75 per cent of the Bible consists of stories. Adding poetry and proverbs, this leaves probably less than 10 per cent abstract 'intellectual' content. Stories help people to interpret and make sense of what happens to them and work out their responses. However, stories are also the ultimate in ambiguous communication because even if the story is enjoyed and appreciated there is no guarantee that it will be understood as you may have hoped it would be. A story, by definition, can be interpreted in any number of ways and therefore cannot be relied upon to convey a single theme. The parable of the Good Samaritan was intended to convey good neighbourliness, but was famously reinterpreted by Margaret Thatcher to illustrate the need for sound economics. She made the comment that had the Good Samaritan not had money in his pocket he would not have been able to help the traveller. A story without any interpretation is still a story without any link to an underpinning divine narrative – the story of Jonah being eaten by a fish may to the listener be nothing more than the story of a man being eaten by a fish.

On one occasion I was involved in a residential week for young people who had little or no involvement with the Church and were not familiar with the Gospel stories. They were a group of young people that we knew well and they had indicated that they were happy for us to arrange and put on a late night 'God slot'. This 'God slot' would start just before midnight and go on for half an hour, or for as long as the young people wanted to stay. We would put out cushions, play chilled-out music and project images onto the wall through a video screen. Some nights the young people would bring their own music and we would sit around listening to their tunes.

Each evening we would tell one of the parables in an updated form. It fell to me to retell the parable of the Prodigal Son and this was the story I told:

A mother with a ten-year-old son was left by her husband after 20 years of marriage. The father ran his own business and set himself up in a prosperous new area with his new partner. The mother had to move to a smaller house and get a job for the first time since she and her husband were married. Soon she was stressed out by trying to balance the demands of her job, her home and her son, and was struggling with a lack of self-esteem after what had happened. The father, however, felt he had a new lease of life in a new home with a new partner. The son began to enjoy the weekends with his father while feeling quite oppressed by the time he spent with his mum. To him it seemed that his mother was always 'on his case' and nagging him about something. By contrast his father seemed relaxed and able to enjoy himself.

Eventually, the son asked his mother if he could go and live with his father. She was clearly upset but was not going to say 'no' if that was what he wanted. It was only once the son started to live with his father that he began properly to understand the situation. The reality was that his father was self-centred and not really concerned with the needs of a ten-year-old and with the demands of school life. His mother might have got annoyed with him if he did not do his homework, but his father might not even remember to send him to school with a packed lunch. His mother might have insisted that he was in bed with his light out by nine o'clock, but his father would not necessarily even be back from work in time to say goodnight to him.

The reality was that his mother loved him with all her heart. By contrast, his father loved having him around, but maybe only as an accessory in the 'perfect life' that he was building up for himself. The boy felt horrified at the hurt he must have done to his mother and felt for a long time that he could not face her. Eventually after a particularly difficult evening with his father he felt that he could stand it no longer. It was the weekend, and he had wanted to get out and play. Instead he had to sit quietly and pretend he was not there while his father entertained business clients. He decided to go and throw himself on the mercy of his mother. 'At least while I am there I feel as if I have a voice of my own,' he thought. The boy didn't say a word to anyone but just put himself on a train and turned up at his mother's home. Of course, she was thrilled to see him.

Following the story there was a moment's silence. Then Simon, one of the young people, spoke up: 'That's me, that's my life!' There were two salutary points about his response. One

81

was that it connected with his own situation. The power of telling stories lies in the fact that the people listening are able to become the interpreters, translating the story into their own context and working out what they think. Telling the story meant that Simon had a chance to use the raw stuff of his day-to-day living to make his response. The story was effective in the way that it had allowed him to connect with his own personal story, helped him recognize and appreciate the love and support of his mother and, even if only for a moment, enabled him to make some sense of his life and place in the world.

> Because it can give coherent shape to human events and make human actions understandable, narrative form helps people to feel they understand the world . . . human beings call upon the narrative form when they need to present a meaningful account of experience to themselves and others. (Sterk, 1993:192)

The second point to Simon's response was that, while the story clearly connected with Simon's situation, he did not make any attempt to pursue his interest. This was partly because he did not want to but partly also because he did not know how to do so. He was interested in the fact that the story reflected his life situation, but his interest was no different from what he might have felt if the plot in a film had reflected a familiar situation.

He did not know how he might pursue an interest, had he wanted to do so. This was because there was no template in his mind to map out the set of possible responses that he might make to a story from the Bible. We had assumed that there would be a connecting narrative in his mind and that his response to the story would lead to a subsequent reflection about Christianity. We had hoped that if that story resonated with him, he might want to explore other stories. The retelling of the parable, however, was the limit of his knowledge base about Christianity, and so the story was heard as just a story and not (as it was to us) as a part of the underlying narrative about the nature of God.

A comparable story to this one was told to me by a friend, Debbie, about her neighbour Jane, a young lady in her twenties who moved out of the family home when her mother died unexpectedly. The house was let for the year to an overtly Christian tenant who stuck religious imagery on the walls. When the young lady moved back into the family home after the year away, it transpired that the lodger had left a poster of the 'Footprints' poem on the wall. The poster caught her attention because the poem had been read at her mother's funeral. Debbie wondered whether the fact that the same poem that had been read at her mother's funeral had been left on her living-room wall might stimulate Jane to think more deeply about the sentiments expressed. As Jane was someone who had recently been through a difficult time, Debbie had thought it might possibly lead her to consider the nature of the God referred to in the poem as someone who will carry us when life is hard. For Jane, however, the significance of the poster being on her wall lay simply in its being a 'weird' coincidence. She said that it was 'nice', but she then took the poster off the wall and threw it away. For her, the poem was on the borders of her meaning-map. It was therefore not going to be a trigger to further reflection, but was interpreted only in the light of what she already knew and thought.

Simon's reaction to the story and Jane's reaction to the poem might, at first glance, appear strange. However, they can only be understood through the realization that neither of them had any conceptual framework in which to place the glimpse they had been given of a Christian narrative. When I travelled in Sri Lanka I agreed to spend a day in one of the Buddhist temples teaching English to the local village children. They had photographic memories and could follow a sequence of questions immediately. They could think sequentially in the sense of listing separate and unconnected ideas, but they could not think conceptually in the sense of relating two different ideas to each other. I would ask them what their father did and they would tell me what their father did. I would ask them how many brothers or sisters they had and then they would tell me. They could not, however, make any connections between different questions that I might ask. So they could tell me that they had one brother and one sister. They could tell me that their father worked as a farmer. However, they could not tell me how many children their father had because it involved thinking across from one question to another question, and they did not have adequate conceptual knowledge of the English language to know how the fact that they had two siblings related to the fact that their father would have three children.

A child does not have the conceptual framework to interpret disconnected events. When asked what has happened that day, a child might reply: 'Daddy was angry . . . the bomb went off . . . we had chips.' Simon was not aware of the underpinning Christian story, so there was a limited appreciation of the value of seeing his situation reflected in an updated reworked version of a parable. I had been working on the assumption that Simon would know something of the scriptural narrative and would recognize that in touching the hem of a biblical story, he was also touching the cloak. I had hoped that once he had recognized that the biblical narrative echoed his situation, he would automatically be encouraged to look for more insights and connective comments. But the knowledge he had of Bible stories was only as isolated fragments, and so he did not interpret the reworked parable of the Prodigal Son as a part of a wider dialogue, as I had hoped he might. The story was just a story. The same might be true of other Bible stories for other people, for example a young person being bullied at school is not automatically going to be reassured by the fact that Joseph was bullied by his brothers (Genesis 37.4) – telling someone who is being bullied a story of someone else being bullied is not necessarily going to help them.

Even in contexts where young people might be attending church youth groups and have the opportunity to learn about the Christian faith, it is not necessarily the case that they will be chatting about what they have learnt with their friends at school. This means that their understanding of Christianity can often be random pieces of knowledge without context or application. The task of a young person coming to terms with the claims of Christianity is comparable to the role of the actor in coming to terms with a character in a play. Rylance (1992) talked about how it was only after 80 or 90 performances that he could properly internalize and understand the role of Hamlet:

> Because you could learn it, but you couldn't make sense of it until you experienced it . . . There is no way you can do it with dictionary or rational thought. It is only through play that you get there. (Rylance, 1992:33)

The Use of Understatement

The previous chapter suggested that when I talk about God I am likely, at least in the first instance, to be misunderstood. This means that I want people to come back on what I have said and ask questions in order to clarify and work through what they have heard me saying. Storytelling has an inherent element of understatement in that stories are told on the assumption that the reaction of people listening is as important as the narrative of the person speaking. A story is squeezed of life if it has to be explained because stories allow people to participate in the interpretation. When I learnt to write poetry I was told that a poem should come out of the silence and go back into the silence. It is the same as with humour in that you cannot explain a joke. Humour and poetry stop being humour and poetry once they are explained or introduced because people's responses are being pre-set in the telling. It is the nature of humour, poetry and story, as it is of the gospel, that people respond as they wish. To allow people space to respond as they wish needs me to practise the art of understatement and to hold myself in check.

A judicious detachment is integral to any work with people. As the course director for the Centre for Youth Ministry (CYM) course in Cambridge, I once worked with a student who thanked me for the support that I had given her during a difficult period.

She said to me that she did not think that she would have survived without that support. 'The thing is,' she said, 'when it was all finished, who was there left for me to get angry with?' It is a thin dividing line between wanting to offer someone support and wanting to be popular and liked. In crossing this dividing line I had, maybe, taken away from her some of her ability to deal with the situation on her own.

A careful use of understatement allows the listener to interpret what you might be saying. The power of an understatement is that it allows people to reach out for what might be inaccessible or inexpressible and to grasp it for themselves. In *The Little Prince* (De Saint-Exupéry, 2002) the fox explains to the prince that it is only with the heart that one can see rightly; what is essential is invisible to the eye. The prince has spent a long time looking after a single rose and it is the time that the prince wasted on looking after his rose that has made the rose so important. Claudio Ranieri, football manager of Chelsea in 2004, quoted *The Little Prince* to explain his philosophy of football management. Ranieri talked about how the unseen qualities in a footballer were the most important. He argued that there was only a limited amount that skill or fitness levels could be improved in a footballer; psychology and a will to win is where most improvement could be made.

A different angle on the idea of understatement is to take the concept of using negative spaces. The artist's version of this, as explained to me by a graphic designer, is that if I wanted to draw a glass I would shade in the area round the glass and the space that was left would be the shape of the glass. Or, musically it is the pauses between the beats that define the beats and not the beats that define the pauses. It is because I live in a loud and noisy world that I can make the assumption that life is in fact noise interspersed with silence. The reality, though, is that I live in a world of silence interspersed with noise. The wife of a friend of mine would always talk in negative spaces and mean more by what she did not say than by what she did say. I learnt to notice the gaps in her conversation as the indicators of what she really meant. If she told me that her child was happy at school and that she was seeing a lot of her friends then I would guess at the fact that her husband was probably working long hours. If she told me that her husband was well and that her child was happy, I would ask about her friends.

Irony and understatement abound in biblical texts from Sarah's laughter, to David beating Goliath, to the sufferings of Job, to the mystery of the virgin birth. Whole swathes of New Testament interpretation would be lost if what is not said is over-looked. The idea of negative spaces can unlock some familiar stories in Scripture:

- The story of the feeding of the 5,000 (Luke 9.10ff.) follows immediately on from Jesus being told by the disciples of John the Baptist that John had been beheaded by Herod. Jesus then immediately withdrew to the wilderness. The crowd followed him and what followed was the miraculous feeding. The story acquires a whole extra level of meaning if it is recognized that Jesus withdrew because he was upset at the news about John.
- In the story of the woman caught in adultery, the crucial missing detail is the man who was also (presumably) caught in adultery (John 8). Why is she brought before Jesus, and not him too?
- One of the few jokes in the New Testament can be lost if you do not notice the negative space in what Peter says at the day of Pentecost: 'These men are not drunk, as you suppose. It's only nine in the morning!' (Acts 2.15). In other words, at 9 a.m. you haven't had the opportunity to get drunk, so how could we be?
- There is a clear negative space between Acts 9.18 and Acts 9.20. The impression given in the Acts account seems to suggest that Paul was converted and then immediately spent several days with the disciples in Damascus. However, it is in Galatians that the reader is told that there was a three-year gap between his conversion and his starting to preach (Galatioans 1.16–18). He withdrew to the deserts of Arabia to make sense of the vision he had seen.

- Jesus appears to his brother James (1 Corinthians 15.7) after his resurrection. But earlier, his family thought him mad and tried to restrain him (Mark 3.21) and his brothers did not believe him (John 7.5). Thus the idea of Jesus wanting to explain his Messiahship to a family that neither understood him nor believed him adds a poignancy to the resurrection story.

As in *The Little Prince,* where what is essential is invisible to the eye, so in the gospel it is the parts that are not readily accessible which can provide a key to unlocking people's imagination.

The Use of Dialogue

Dialogue is commended in Scripture. 'Come, let us dialogue together' God said to the Israelites (see Isaiah 1.18). Paul stayed for three months debating in the synagogue (Acts 20.3). Dialogue, though, like 'spiritual', is another word that has suffered from overuse and is often used to mean simply 'conversation'. The idea of dialogue is derived from Greek and Latin words meaning 'to speak alternately'. Dialogue is properly used to refer to a formal discussion or negotiation, especially between opposing sides in a political or international context. Ambiguity creates the need for dialogue.

In a dialogue, each person tries to understand where the other person is coming from. If I am dialoguing with someone, I am less interested in people's conclusions than in how they reached them. In the film *Tomorrow Never Dies,* James Bond is up against Carver, the media mogul, who is deliberately manipulating world events so that his paper is in a position to report first on what is happening. Carver says to Bond that he has never forgotten the lesson taught to him by his first editor, which is that the most important feature of a story is not 'who' or 'where' or 'what' but 'why'. In a conversation it is most important not to reflect on what someone does but on why they do it.

The foundations of true dialogue are 'humility' and 'compromise'. The history of the word humility and the current usage of the word 'compromise' illustrate how people are not naturally comfortable with the idea of dialogue and listening to alternative points of view. The Bible was written in *koiné* or common Greek. *Koiné* emerged after the conquests of Alexander the Great (roughly 336–323 BCE) when Greek became the standard language of commerce and government. It existed alongside many local languages and was adopted as a second language by the native people of these regions. *Koiné* Greek was a standardized, simplified version of classical Greek. There was no word in either classical or *koiné* Greek to express the idea of humility that did not have negative connotations. Therefore a word had to be invented, and the word used in the Scriptures for humility makes its first appearance there.

In a similar way there is no word in contemporary English usage meaning 'compromise' that has entirely positive connotations. If someone is seen to have compromised, they are seen to have given something away and it is usually understood as a negative transaction. The essence of a compromise, however, is when two people come together and each of them takes on board some of what the other person has said. This is a good and honourable thing, but there is no word in the English language that adequately describes the process. The synonyms for compromise on the Word 2002 computer program are: cooperation, negotiation, concession, conciliation, finding the middle ground, give and take, settlement. Agreement (as in making an agreement, not coming to one) has positive connotations because it conjures up the image of two sides putting forward their positive sides to join in the middle. The language also gets closer to a positive sense when the word 'compromise' is used as a noun rather than as a verb – 'to reach a compromise' is considered as a more valiant endeavour than simply 'to compromise', which is seen as selling out or capitulation.

Nelson Mandela undercut any negative perception of compromise when, on being released from prison after 26 years, he talked about the need to be prepared to compromise his most basic principles. I remember being amazed by his comment because I thought of principles as things that one upheld or defended but not things that one compromised. Mandela was true to his word, and at the Truth and Reconciliation Commission people would sit on the seats and pray for the talks to take place that day. South African democracy was born. My friend Eddie said that he would always compromise himself for his family and friends. 'I am on your side – what is the argument?' was his approach, if I was in any trouble or need of assistance.

Compromise is rarely the easy option. People usually prefer to have choices made into a simple dichotomy – things are either 'right' or 'wrong'; the answer is either 'yes' or 'no'; it is either 'this way' or 'that way'. Simplifying a situation in this way tends to make people feel more secure. However, the desire to reduce things to two options can often misrepresent what the situation might be – things are rarely ever entirely one thing or the other, but are generally a combination of both. In reality, choices are always made with a combination of motives and therefore decisions are likely to incorporate a variety of options.

I am not using the idea of compromise to refer to the content of the gospel but instead to the way in which the gospel message is communicated. It is a methodological rather than a substantive issue – it is not just what I do or say but also the way that I do or say it. There are a number of examples of compromise written into the pages of Scripture.

- The Pharisee and the tax collector (Luke 18.9–14) go into the temple to pray and it is the tax collector who beats his breast, saying, 'God have mercy on me, a sinner' and who goes away feeling justified.
- Abraham haggles with God over the destruction of Sodom and Gomorrah (Genesis 18.22–33) – he agrees not to destroy the city for firstly 50, then 45, then 40, then 30 and finally 20 righteous people.

- Moses compromises because the people were hard-hearted and stubborn (Mark 10.5) and allows a man to write a certificate of divorce because a woman had become displeasing to him (Deuteronomy 24.1).

- Hosea is asked to live with the fact that his wife has committed adultery (Hosea 3.1).

- In Isaiah (30.21) God tells the Israelites that whether they turn to the right or to the left they will hear a voice saying, 'This is the way; walk in it'.

- The Syro-Phoenician woman haggles with Jesus and persuades him to heal her daughter when initially he had been unwilling (Mark 7.29).

- When Jesus casts the demons out of Legion, the demons beg him not to send them into the abyss. He gives them permission to go into a herd of pigs and the herd rushes down the steep bank of the lake and is destroyed (Luke 8.26–35).

- When Paul is asked about whether it is wrong to eat meat offered to idols, the gist of his reply is: you know that it is all right, I know that it is all right, but we do not want to trip people up. Everything is permissible but not everything is possible (1 Corinthians 10.23).

- Jesus suggests that it is better to leave an evil spirit in place than to clean out the house, leave it empty and run the risk of the evil spirit returning with seven other spirits more wicked than itself (Luke 11.24–26).

- The parable of the weeds (Matthew 13.24–30) talks of weeds left growing alongside the wheat until the harvest. This seems to suggest that if things are left as they are then an appropriate time for resolution will present itself. Time is a powerful agent of the Holy Spirit.

- The parable of the unjust steward tells of a man who knew he was going to get sacked and so wrote off debts owed to his master in order to secure his own future employment. The master commended him on the basis that he had acted shrewdly and used his master's money to gain friends for himself (Luke 16.8).

The late Bishop Lesslie Newbiggin's reflection on the story of Jesus entering into Jerusalem (Mark 11.1–11) provides an illustration of how the most straightforward options are not necessarily the best ways of responding to a situation. The Romans were an occupying power in a foreign country. One logical response to the situation was to oppose it (as did the Zealots). The Zealots were a Jewish religious–political faction of Judea, existing for about 70 years in the first century. Their doctrines had a strong focus on the necessity of violent actions against the enemies of Judaism. The Zealots could not accept any foreign rule or domination as they believed that the land of the Jews, Judea, could be ruled only according to principles and authority of God. According to Luke 6.15, Simon, one of Jesus' disciples, was a Zealot. The response of the Zealots, therefore, was to take responsibility on themselves to sort a situation out. The second logical response to the situation was live it (as did the Essenes). The Essenes were a Jewish ascetic sect of which John the Baptist was a member. Their view of the world seemed to be one of predeterminism. Their eternal and omnipotent God not only knew everything that would occur in the world but also arranged for it to happen. Therefore it was not for them to intervene in political affairs. They lived together in a shared community and all who joined gave away or sold their worldly goods and gave the profits to the leaders of the community. It is sometimes wondered whether Christ was an Essene because he criticized the Scribes and Pharisees, but never the Essenes. The response of the Essenes was to accept the situation and to leave the responsibility to God. Jesus' response, in fact, followed neither course, but he rode into Jerusalem riding on a donkey and the crowds proclaimed him as the King of the Jews. This approach contains both the challenge within the Zealot perspective and the acceptance within the Essene perspective.

The strength of feelings in the church over some issues can leave me feeling uneasy with any idea of compromise, often simply because I am frightened of getting things wrong. Paul was prepared to accommodate his approach when he had Timothy circumcised because the Jews in that area knew that his father was Greek (Acts 16.3). Compromise involves a willingness to identify what are 'negotiables' and what are 'non-negotiables' of the Christian faith. There is an urgency to this task because it is always easier to add on to the non-negotiables to make sure that nothing is missed out. This is the trap that Eve falls into when the serpent asks her whether God had really said that she should not eat from the tree nor should she touch it (Genesis 3.1–3). The serpent is careful not to disagree with anything that God had said but instead to add on to what God had said. In this way to Eve's untutored ear it can appear as if he is agreeing and suggesting even more. In a context where people do not have a framework of the gospel there is a responsibility to be clear about what does and does not need to be said. If I present negotiables as non-negotiables then I have set (my own) sanctification ahead of (other people's) redemption.

5

The Ambiguous Evangelist as Fool of Christ

In Chapter 3 it was suggested that language cannot adequately express ideas about God. This is because making a statement about Jesus might be intended as a truth claim but will be heard as a statement of preference or choice. Communicating the gospel as something other than one of a range of options means presenting it in a way that might not fit comfortably with many people's existing ideas. To present the gospel as truth (through word or action) may mean that people are startled or even shocked. This chapter now explores what form 'being startled' might take. It looks at the reasons why Jesus spoke in parables and what the idea of the 'fool' can bring to evangelism.

The Power of Parables

Jesus was the original ambiguous evangelist. He said that the point of using parables was to present ideas in such a way that people will listen and listen but not understand; they will look and look but will not learn (Matthew 13.14). Jesus' use of parables sets up a paradigm of engagement in which people have to ask if they wanted an explanation: 'Those who understand will be given more' (see Matthew 13.12). When the disciples asked Jesus why he spoke in parables, he replied that to those outside, everything was given in parables so that 'they may be ever seeing but never perceiving, and ever hearing but never understanding; otherwise they might turn and be forgiven!' (Mark 4.12).

There are three separate ideas behind this dynamic of offering ideas in storytelling form. Each can contribute to an understanding of ambiguous evangelism.

First, by using parables, Jesus was able to introduce themes in a new context. When Jesus was asked about who his neighbour was (Luke 10.29), he told the story of the Good Samaritan. It was a way of giving the listeners ideas and images in bite-size chunks that they could then make sense of. They could engage with a subject without necessarily realizing the process they were involved in. A parable, in this sense, is a story that provides a new and safe context for the listener to work a set of thoughts through to a conclusion. A parable is also a way of turning an issue on its head so that it can be rethought and looked at from another angle. The first poem I ever wrote was a single line:

I
saw
a
daffodil
on
a
rubbish
tip

This poem was parabolic in the sense that it was taking a small illustration to make a wider point.

In the Old Testament, there is the parable told by Nathan to David. David sent Bathsheba's husband, Uriah the Hittite, into the front line of a war, knowing full well he would be killed. Once Uriah was dead, David was then free to marry his widow. God's response to David's sin came through the prophet Nathan, who told David a parable about a lamb (2 Samuel 12). When David heard the story he was outraged at the rich man taking the poor man's lamb to feed his guest. Unknowingly, David was coaxed into an arena of thinking where he would be confronted with the thought processes that lay behind his own actions. Once he realized that his actions towards Bathsheba were equivalent to the rich man's actions towards the poor man's lamb, he was able to repent and begin appropriate remediation.

There is a parallel process when, in a soap opera or film, a storyline triggers memories for someone watching. A viewer who is or who has been in the same situation as the screen character may start thinking about how they themselves have dealt with it. When sensitive issues such as domestic abuse or rape are the subject of television soaps, helpline details are given at the end of the programme for viewers who have been affected by what has happened in that episode.

The second reason behind Jesus' use of parables is that the reality of God's truth is too powerful and too big to be absorbed in one telling. Since the 'foolishness of God' is wiser than human wisdom (1 Corinthians 1.25), storytelling is a means for people to be eased into realizing the truth about God in an incremental way. After a succession of jaded and repetitive church services, it is easy to underestimate the power and majesty of God. But the Bible gives examples of people whose experience of God is clearly transcendent and hard to bear. In each of the examples below, awareness of God results in a consciousness of sin.

- Isaiah (6.5) in the vision in the temple said, 'Woe to me! I am ruined! For I am a man of unclean lips, and I live among a people of unclean lips, and my eyes have seen the King, the LORD Almighty.'
- Simon Peter fell at Jesus' knees and said, 'Go away from me, Lord; I am a sinful man!' (Luke 5.8).
- Amos talked about the wrath of God in delivering up the city. The assumption behind what Amos said is that the people must have done something wrong for the city to have been destroyed. Therefore they should not call out to the Lord because he has been the judge of their sins.

If ten men are left in one house, they too will die. And if a relative who is to burn the bodies comes to carry them out of the house and asks anyone still hiding there, 'Is anyone with you?' and he says 'No,' then he will say 'Hush! We must not mention the name of the LORD' (Amos 6.9–10).

- When Moses went up to the top of Mount Sinai, he had to warn people not to force their way through to try and see the Lord because if they did so they would perish (Exodus 19.21).

In using parables Jesus was not deliberately trying to confuse people. There was no advantage in him making people feel unintelligent in order to make a point. Rather, he was being pragmatically kind by not giving people too much truth too quickly – because they would simply not be able to assimilate it. This is the idea alluded to in the saying, 'Do not throw your pearls to pigs. If you do, they may trample them under their feet, and then turn and tear you to pieces' (Matthew 7.6).

The third reason for using parables is to help people to realize that they do not understand an issue. Parables are a method of provoking curiosity in order to arouse interest. Isaiah dramatized his message by walking naked and barefoot (Isaiah 20); Jeremiah smashed pots (Jeremiah 19) and Ahijah tore his coats into twelve pieces (1 Kings 11.29–31). If a parable makes someone realize that they do not know everything about a person or situation, then they may be stimulated into wanting to find out more. It is this third reason for parables that is most akin to the idea of ambiguous evangelism.

I worked for three years as the chaplain at London South Bank University. South Bank was a large multi-campus site with around 18,000 students. I had one room and no immediate role in the life of the university. My initial task was to make people realize that there was a chaplain in place. I had to deal with the fact that there was no understanding in many people's minds of what a chaplain might do – but could only do so after they had realized that there was someone there at all. I had no publicity budget and I felt that I was never going to manage to communicate clearly to a large and transitory student population. There were some people who would always come along and there were others who were never going to come. If all I did was to communicate a clear and comprehensive picture of the services on offer in the chaplaincy, then it would have brought me to the attention of people who were potentially interested in any case and therefore would probably have found me anyway. It would probably also have confirmed in the minds of the others why they would not choose to access the services of a chaplaincy. I wanted to connect with some of those 'others' and give them just enough awareness to make them think of making further enquiries. So I set out to present the work of the chaplaincy creatively and ambiguously.

On one occasion, I performed a play-parable by setting myself up with all the equipment needed to clean people's shoes. Formally dressed in black suit and clerical shirt, I presented myself as a caricature of a priest. People were intrigued, amused and confused. When asked why I was doing this, I would deliberately reply enigmatically. I would tell people that it was 'all part of the service'. My cleaning people's shoes while dressed up in full clerical garb was an acted-out parable, the point of which was not to explain what I was doing but to leave people intrigued enough to wonder and to ask further questions. Over the three years, I used various other pieces of ambiguous communication. I took photographs of a biscuit and used it on a poster with the words '@ The Chaplaincy'. I did email-shots to staff and students using the words of poems such as Stevie Smith's 'Not waving but drowning'. When the kettle was stolen from the chaplaincy, I put up 300 notices around the university saying, 'God knows who has got the kettle!' I created different designs for the writing paper I used. One design had an image of a priest-clown in a dog collar; another was with a spoof press release: SHOCK HORROR! VICAR FOUND DOING HIS JOB!

By providing the optimum level of information and insight, people can choose either to pursue an interest or else to walk away from what they have heard. David Attenborough said on

Desert Island Discs (1999) that the best way to get someone interested in a subject is to show a great energy combined with a great ignorance. There is a lightness of touch assumed within this approach that does not leave people feeling disempowered or judged, but instead allows them to come back to ask about what they hear as being said. When the disciples of John the Baptist come to ask Jesus if he is 'the one who was to come' or whether they should expect another (Luke 7.19), Jesus does not give them a point-by-point explanation but tells them to look around and to draw conclusions from what they see.

I use the idea of the fool to provide a framework for this enigmatic, ambiguous approach to truth-telling, where people are encouraged to search things out for themselves rather than having everything laid out in one single sweep. The fool in this sense is most emphatically not a weak figure, the object of people's mirth and scorn. Rather, it is a figure in the mould of the fool as found in *King Lear*. In this tragedy, there are only three characters with the ability to stand up to the king: Cordelia, the Duke of Kent and the fool. The fool is the most intelligent, insightful and clear-thinking character in the play. He has honesty and integrity, and is loyal to the bitter end. It is also the fool who provides the few instances of humour and amusement in the play.

The fool is a character in whom seriousness of content and lightness of manner are found hand-in-hand. In the same way, the Christian point of view can be offered with lightness of touch – as suggestion or insight, rather than as direction or command. Hull (1999) talked about an illuminating rather than an adjudicating role of religion. Being able to put a point of view well is an art form that depends on an ability to make your opinion known but not in such a way that people would feel constrained in responding. This is what Jesus was hinting at with his enigmatic response to the question of why he spoke in parables. Through these stories, he was providing just the right amount and level of information so that people could decide either to choose to pursue an interest or else to walk away from what they had heard.

There are distinctive features of how one might take the role of the fool in conversation.

The Fool Allows Himself to be Misunderstood

I once begged a father not to try to over-identify with his 12-year-old daughter by telling her that he liked the music of the rapper Eminem. I wanted him to understand that if he moved onto her territory and said how much he liked Eminem, she would then need to move further on to find her own space. It is self-evident that young people do not always welcome over-identification from an older person – even if they are wanting to show that they understand the issues of life from a young perspective. It is sometimes the role of the adult to allow young people to react against their position so that they are then able to work out what they think themselves. Often, young people appreciate the chance to listen to and learn from someone else's view on life. 'I don't like being so old and unable to keep up with all you are doing,' my grandmother once said to me. 'Granny,' I replied with all the precocious certainty of a teenager, 'it is my job to be young and it is your job to be old.'

Observing a youth-work colleague involved in an animated discussion with a young person, I later asked her what the discussion was about. She said that the young person had a friend who had been excluded from a youth club the previous week and he had not understood the reasons why this had happened. I suggested to the youth worker that there is a thin dividing line between explaining something and justifying something. I felt that in this context the young person had the right to form his own conclusions about the reasons for his friend's exclusion. Sometimes when I am wanting to explain a situation or make myself understood, I feel that what I am actually doing is trying to make people like me. If I imagine myself in the place of Jesus in the conversation with the rich young man, I can never see myself as having the confidence to let him walk away sadly

(Matthew 19.22). I would have wanted to run after him and to explain things differently so that he might be able to accommodate his wealth *and* a commitment to the kingdom.

Being prepared to let someone form their own conclusions requires a lot of strength and self-awareness. Jesus was a good example of someone who allowed himself to be misunderstood. He knew too well that people would not understand the nature of Messiahship that he was offering. He worked determinedly to try to prevent people misrepresenting him, for example by asking people who had been healed to keep quiet (Mark 7.36). Only when Peter finally recognized the true nature of his Messiahship did Jesus begin to teach systematically about what was going to happen to him. But still he knew that he would be executed as a direct result of the authorities' misunderstanding of what he had to say. Despite this knowledge, he resolutely set his face towards Jerusalem and his crucifixion.

The Fool Allows Himself to be Considered Different

It is often easier for someone to talk intimately to a comparative stranger than to a friend. Sometimes people will disclose information more readily to someone who is not 'up close and personal'. A certain distance is required for a particular quality of exchange. Similarly, I also find that people will feel secure in talking if they are confident that if they meet me again in a different context, the conversation will not be referred to. Their confidence in the relationship comes from feeling comfortable that there is both an appropriate distance as well as an appropriate intimacy. If I am going to play the fool, I cannot mind when people want to keep a certain distance if that is what will enable them to be vulnerable or honest with me. On some occasions I have had people talk to me about sensitive issues and then avoid me the next day.

Towards the end of a three-year period working for a church in Luton, I was informed by a member of the congregation that people liked me because I was not like them. I was only living in the parish for a limited period of time, so there was a level of identification and belonging that I could not offer. I could, however, bring a different thought process, a different understanding and a different view on life. Equally though, it seemed that it was at the point at which the spaces and the gaps in the relationship were recognized that the strengths and connections could also be acknowledged.

Educational philosophy describes how, when potential points of disagreement are opened up, it produces a dialectical tension which allows for the possibility of a later fuller agreement. If people can be made aware of where points of disparity might emerge, then the possibility for dialogue and understanding is created. When the Syro-Phoenician woman asked Jesus to heal her daughter, he replied that food should not be taken from the children and given to the dogs (Mark 7.27). The words on their own could sound harsh. Jesus was saying that his primary mission was to the Jews, but in doing this he was comparing the Jews to children and the Syro-Phoenicians to dogs. Presumably though, there was something in his tone that reassured the woman, because in drawing her attention to the difference between the two of them, he made her realize what she could then ask of him. This is an illustration of the understood/not understood nature of ambiguity that is inherent in confronting someone with the reality of the claims of Christ.

When I was a student I would be taken out for regular meals by an elderly friend. As I sat trying to decide what to eat, Patricia would suggest to me the most expensive dish on the menu. She would say, 'I quite fancy the steak, what about you?' I knew that she would never choose the expensive steak for herself. But in referring to it she was, in effect, giving me permission to choose whatever I wanted up to the price of the steak. I liked the way that, in doing this, she opened up for me the possibility of choice.

Hosea is told by God to allow himself to be made a fool of. He is told to take back his wife even though she is an adulteress and loved by another (Hosea 3.1). On one level, Hosea is horribly humiliated because he has been shown up and cuckolded in public. On another level, for him to take back Gomer, the wife who has caused him this pain, is such a radical action that it forces the issue of God's love to be rethought. The extremity of the action opens up the space within which the love of God can be considered.

In the film *The Mexican*, Samantha (Julia Roberts) is asked about the nature of commitment. Samantha has a particularly stormy relationship with Jerry (Brad Pitt). The gay hit man she has befriended asks her about her relationship. His question to her is about when two people really love each other but just can't get it together: how do they know when enough is enough? He says:

> In my business you are surrounded by loneliness and finality. Look, I don't know what your thinking is of an afterlife, but when people die it is scary and they go alone. The people that I send off that have experienced love, they are the less scared. I mean they are still scared, but there is a calmness to them and I think that comes from the knowledge that someone, somewhere loved them and cared for them and will miss them. Now I see that from time to time and I am awed by it. I don't think I would be telling you any of this if it wasn't for Frank. Anyway it is a loaded question. When two people love each other, totally, truthfully, all the way love each other, the answer to that question is simple, especially in your case. When do you get to the point where enough is enough? Never, never.

It is not an easy stance to take. Amos, Jonah and Jeremiah all felt, at different times, exposed and made angry by the isolation required in representing God's message. Jeremiah cursed the day on which he was born (Jeremiah 20.18). Amos felt humiliated at not being taken seriously by Amaziah. Jonah felt that he was made a laughing-stock when his prophecies against Nineveh did not come to fruition.

The Fool is the Perpetual Outsider–Insider

The Christian who is in the world but not of the world (cf. John 15.19) is the fool of God in the sense of always being the outsider–insider in a situation. The fool is the person who never properly fits into a situation. In never fully identifying with any one person, the fool is free to identify with everyone. If I am going to play the fool, I am not always going to fit the expectations that people have of me. When I worked as a curate in Luton, I had a responsibility for conducting the funerals in the parish. I would drive from the parish to the crematorium, followed by the hearse. On one occasion I pulled out into the main road to witness a large car thunder past with music blaring. Quite by chance, the traffic lights ahead immediately changed to red, and so I pulled up alongside this music-pounding, engine-revving machine. In my conventional curate's car, I must have looked the epitome of a sedate and respectable clergyman. I wound down my window and beckoned the driver with my finger. The sight of a dog-collared priest whom he had never seen in his life must have startled him because he slowly and tentatively wound down his own window in response. I leant across and said, with a smile, 'I bury people like you' and then drove away on the green light, leaving him where he was.

On another occasion I had arrived in London on the train from Cambridge and was walking slowly between Kings Cross main line and Kings Cross Thameslink stations. A woman who was working as a prostitute mistook my slow walk as an invitation, walked up to me and propositioned me. I told her that I would have loved to be able to have gone with her but sadly I was unable to because I was an Anglican priest. We chatted for about five minutes. She told me her name, her age and about her family. I was unsure about how to end the conversation. I did not simply want to say 'good luck' because that might be heard as condoning a fraught and difficult way of life. Equally I did not want to hear myself condemning her for the situation she was in. What I did was to take out a £10 note which I gave to her with the words: 'Have 20 minutes off on the Church of England.' I would maintain that here was an instance in which the Christian truth had been communicated in a light-hearted but entirely serious manner.

In the same way there is a close connection between seriousness and laughter. There is a closeness in the extremes of joy and sorrow. This is evidenced in the language of emotions in which one talks of 'crying with laughter' or of 'tears of joy'. Emotions are complex. A friend's father died a few months before his wedding. At the wedding his mother was literally crying tears with joy. She was simultaneously joyful at the wedding and grief-struck that her husband was not there to share in the occasion. The image of the fool allows me to feel comfortable within the complexity of people's different emotions.

My grandmother was so clear and self-aware in the days before her death that I felt proud to be able to actually take the service, being simultaneously grandson and officiating minister. The day after her funeral I took a group of young people motor-cycling as had been arranged some time previously. Thus it was that within 24 hours of burying my grandmother I was in a minibus enjoying the bawdy, jocular hilarity of a group of young people on a trip out. As the fool of Christ, I was participating equally in the sadness of one day and the laughter of the next.

These two occasions were opposite extremes of human emotions but then as the fool, I am going to be comfortable at the extremes of emotions. For me, this is represented by the image of the Pierrot clown, who has a sadness behind the brightly painted face, and a certain grace through what is almost a perfection of clumsiness. Laughing, but with a tear in his eye, he dances with light-footed agility from one situation to another. It is the spiritual poverty of mankind that was to be the Pierrot clown's especial concern (Dick, 1960).

The Fool is the Perpetual Observer

It is the fool in Shakespeare's plays who sees most clearly the truth of what is happening, who speaks out most consistently and directly. In *King Lear*, after the king has settled his inheritance on his two daughters, it is the fool who consistently confronts him with the reality of what he has done. He constantly mirrors back to King Lear the reality of his situation.

Fool: Can'st tell how an oyster makes his shell?
Lear: No.
Fool: Nor I neither, but I can tell why a snail has a house.
Lear: Why?
Fool: Why, to put's head in, not to give it away to his daughters and leave his horns without a case.

The fool is the reminder to Lear of his conscience and the reminder of his better self. He is the most willing and able to speak the truth into the situation. He declares mournfully, 'They'll have me whipped for speaking true, thou'lt have me whipped for lying, and sometimes I am whipped for holding my peace.' Yet it is the fool who is King Lear's loyal companion; when the king is out on the stormy moor exposed to the elements in the bitterly cold storm, there is the fool alongside him.

> He that has and a little tiny wit
> With heigh-ho, the wind and the rain
> Must make content with his fortunes fit . . .

To speak effectively into a situation, the fool has to remain just outside of it. I have never been convinced by one of the prevailing myths of capitalism that you have to experience something to understand it and pass comment upon it. Some of the most mediocre marriage sermons I have heard were by people who were married, and they were mediocre because all they did was to relate their own experiences of marriage. It is often the person outside a situation who sees it most clearly. The Church can see ahead of the rest of society, precisely because it lies behind. It is natural to want to make Christianity accessible by making it relevant. The danger, though, in Christianity perpetually related to the experience of the narrator is that it runs the risk of being exclusive if the listener does not have a parallel set of experiences. For example, churchs that promote married life as a norm can leave single people feeling excluded (Aune, 2002).

Ultimately, however, the fool is the figure of joy. The fool dances the unfettered rhythms of grace. David was a fool when he danced before the ark; wearing a linen ephod he danced before the Lord with all his might. Michal thought his behaviour undignified and David responded by saying that he would celebrate before the Lord and become even more undignified (2 Samuel 6.14–23). It is the fool's playful seriousness and serious playfulness that can companion people in this process. Collins (1994) wrote that

Spiritual joy, that is essential joy, arises from innocence, from purity of consciousness – this is the Fool. The Fool in man is a divine debonair spirit, whose careless empirical gaiety and overflowing mercy embraces life . . . the true priest is a Fool whose purity of life is the folly by which the world grows and is enlightened. (Collins, 1994:74, 76)

6

Styles of Conversation

There are essentially two different approaches I can take when getting involved in a conversation. The first is where I will pick up and follow on from what the other person is saying; for example, someone says that they are feeling tired and I ask if they slept badly the previous night. The other is where I will go off at a tangent to what the other person has said; for example, someone says that they are feeling tired and I might say that I felt tired the other day after I had been to a party. The first approach to conversation is a more linear approach, and the course of the conversation will follow a line of thought through to a conclusion. The second approach is more lateral and here the conversation might follow an idea in different directions. One is not better or worse than the other; they are simply different ways of conducting a conversation and people tend to have a preference for one approach or the other.

I call this the 'blackjack' theory of conversation. In the game of blackjack, the aim is to discard cards in your hand onto the table. This is done either by following a card with a card of the same suit (hearts, clubs, spades, diamonds), or by following a card with a card of the same number. The linear approach to conversation is when I follow suit and continue the subject introduced by the other person. If they talk about their mother's health then I will ask them for how long their mother has not been well. The lateral approach to conversation is when I follow with a card of the same number and if they talk about their mother's health, then I will give a different slant to the conversation and introduce a story about my mother.

Linear thinking is a step-by-step, logical and analytical approach to a situation. Linear thinkers would want to find the most reasonable and direct method of completing a task; thus travelling from point A to point B, they would see a straight line between the two points. They will deviate from that line only if it is unavoidable. 'Lateral' means 'situated at or extending to the side' and lateral thinking is looking at an issue sideways on. Lateral thinking is a term used by De Bono (1973). He defines it as thinking about a problem, even if you have to temporarily ignore misconceptions and obvious solutions.

Caterpillar or Grasshopper?

I call the approach taken in the linear, suit-following style of conversation a 'caterpillar' approach. With caterpillar conversationalists, each thought needs to be chewed over and thought through before progressing onto the next one. I call the approach taken in the lateral, suit-changing style of conversation a 'grasshopper' approach. A grasshopper conversationalist will often jump to a conclusion and then work backwards to understand how they got there. Caterpillars prefer to understand everything in context, to think things through and work out what they mean and then how everything relates to everything else. They tend to think through an idea before they verbalize it. Grasshoppers, on the other hand, like to work through an idea by trying it out and will verbalize an idea in order to work out what they think. They will often jump to the end of a thought-sequence and then work backwards to see how it sounds.

The academic words for these two approaches are deductive thinking (caterpillar) and inductive thinking (grasshopper). Deductive thinkers work top-down and use pre-held thoughts and ideas to interpret the world. They can be thought of as map readers – they look at the map in order to work out the details of the surrounding countryside. This approach is also otherwise known as 'exegesis': taking general principles and applying them systematically to a specific situation. Inductive thinkers, on the other hand, think bottom-up and make patterns out of what they have been thinking rather than fitting their ideas into preformed patterns. Inductive thinkers can be thought of as explorers – they look at the surrounding countryside in order to build up a map in their heads of how things look. This approach is also otherwise known as 'apologetics': different ideas are being followed through on their own merit and not on the basis of how they fit into a wider framework of interpretation.

Matt, as a classic grasshopper, will feel daunted if he reads the strategy manual to a new video game before tinkering with the game first. He might see an explanation of a complex combat system, or try to understand all the new effects different items have, and then panic because none of it makes sense. The best course of action for Matt, as a grasshopper, is to play the game non-committally for a bit first. This means that he can find out what it looks like; he can see some of the ways things are done and laid out and get used to the 'furniture' of the game. When he has a question, he can go back to the manual and work backwards from what he does not understand.

Caterpillars can be avid list makers, map readers and instruction followers. Sam, as a classic caterpillar, has an ambition to own the full set of ordinance survey maps for the whole country. The pleasure for her is connecting what is depicted on the map with what she finds when she visits the place in question. For Sam, maps can have the same appeal as a jigsaw puzzle or crossword in that she is working through how everything fits with everything else.

At worst, grasshoppers and caterpillars misunderstand each other. At best, however, grasshoppers and caterpillars complement each other and work well together. For example, grasshoppers are good at exploring ideas and caterpillars are good at examining their practicality. Grasshoppers can think 'Wouldn't it be nice if . . .?' whereas caterpillars can think, 'What does it mean that . . .?' I, as a classic grasshopper, was having a conversation with Sylvie, who is a classic caterpillar. I told her that a student had invited us to visit him and his wife in Zimbabwe. I made the comment intending to convey pleasure at being invited. She replied cautiously, thinking through the practicalities of what such a trip might involve.

Chris, my line manager, an easy-going, deceptively intelligent man, is a classic caterpillar. I have joked with him that if I want to get my way in a meeting then I need to have introduced my point within the first five minutes because at that point he would not yet have grasped all the detail and worked out what it was that he might be agreeing to. His riposte was that if he wanted to get me to agree to something then all he needed to do was to wait 20 minutes because by that point I would have heard too much detail, would probably be bored by the conversation and want to get onto something else.

A caterpillar or a grasshopper approach to conversation is a technique, not an ability. In other words, while each person is likely to be either a more natural caterpillar or a grasshopper-type, it is possible to learn either approach and not to be tied to a personal aptitude or preference for one or the other. You can adapt your approach to what the situation might require. The Church, as an institution, loves to divide people into caterpillars or grasshoppers. Caterpillars are labelled as practical people and are considered to be good at management and organization. Grasshoppers are labelled as intuitive and imaginative people and are considered to be good at vision and leadership. Chris, who would recognize himself as a caterpillar, would argue strongly against keeping the two of them separate – his opinion is that managers sometimes have to lead and leaders always have to manage. In other words he is suggesting that caterpillars have to learn to grasshopper when appropriate, and similarly the other way round.

A Grasshopper Approach to Evangelism

My suggestion is that Jesus tended to be a caterpillar when in conversation with the disciples and when he wanted people to understand what he was saying. An example of this came when Simon asked Jesus how often he should forgive someone (Matthew 18.21). Jesus replied with a straightforward, logical answer. However, in conversation with the crowds and when he wanted to challenge and provoke, Jesus tended to be a grasshopper. When the Pharisees complained that Jesus welcomed sinners and ate with them, Jesus told them a parable about someone with a hundred sheep who loses one of them (Luke 15.3). The connection between the two is not immediately apparent because Jesus did not answer in a logical and linear manner.

The implication for ambiguous evangelism, therefore, is that the caterpillar approach is what is needed in church on Sundays or in a midweek house group, but a grasshopper approach is going to be more effective with people who do not know anything of the Christian faith. In a church service, people have the same perspective, which is that they have come together to worship God. What is needed, therefore, is explanation and application of a Christian message. In a work context, or a student context, or a mother and toddlers group, or any other situation outside the Church, people have a variety of perspectives. What is needed here, therefore, is an approach to conversation that resonates with them – but also allows the conversation to go in different directions.

There is an extent to which the Christian constituency is conditioned to expect conversations about the Christian faith to be careful and considered. It is assumed that there will be time for people to put forward their opinion and time for people to respond. However, the reality is that when opportunities to talk about the Christian faith arise, they are often likely to be in the form of quick, conversational snapshots. Often there is simply not the space to sit and make a considered response to an issue and to explain how it fits within the grand meta-narrative of the

Christian story. Rachel, a schoolteacher, said that when she was in the staffroom for coffee she might have only a matter of seconds to feed her opinion into the discussion. Similarly, a student in the pub with friends might have just one brief opportunity to talk about the faith during a whole evening.

When Brazil won the World Cup in 2002, a number of the team fell to their knees on the pitch praying in gratitude for their victory; three Brazilian players removed their famous yellow shirts to reveal undershirts that declared 'Jesus loves me' and 'I belong to Jesus'. Behind this striking image was the conviction of the team chaplain that because the media did not want to hear them talk about Christianity, they had to speak about their faith in sound bites. The idea of sound bites is not that Christians should ape political parties with pithy aphorisms. Rather, it is that Christians should be ready to use short and provocative comments that might tease or provoke people's interest. The chaplain of the Brazilian football team reckoned that any comment on Christianity by a member of the team needed to be completed in as long a time as it would take a match to flare without it burning the holder's fingers.

A grasshopper approach does not automatically mean that there is a logical sequence of ideas or a coherent story-line that is being followed. *Pulse Media* and *MTV* are examples of fast-paced shows which have images and concepts ricocheting around the screen in different directions. It is a distinctly grasshopper style of presentation. The film *Moulin Rouge* takes the same approach, and although there is a deliberate move away from a logical sequential narrative, it still follows a story-line. The poet (Ewan McGregor) falls for a beautiful courtesan (Nicole Kidman) whom the jealous duke covets. The narrative unfolds through a deluge of ideas and an eclectic collection of music.

It is a simple but obvious point that if I am having a conversation with someone who does not have a working knowledge of Christianity, then by definition the conversation will never be about Christ unless I introduce the subject. If I am only ever a caterpillar in conversations and follow on from what the other person is saying, then a Christian perspective on the situation will never emerge. So I need to learn the skills of being a grasshopper and adopting a lateral approach to conversation; I need to 'play a card of the same number' rather than 'playing a card of the same suit' in order to introduce a Christian perspective to the conversation, when it is appropriate. One example of taking a grasshopper approach is offering to pray for someone, and this is often appreciated and heard as helpful and supportive by someone without any Christian framework or belief structure.

Jesus was often in grasshopper mode when talking with the crowds. When he was anointed by the sinful woman (Luke 7.36–50), the Pharisees asked Jesus if he knew the type of woman she was. If Jesus had followed suit and answered in a linear fashion, he would have assured them that he did know the type of woman she was, but the conversation would then have been heading straight down the cul-de-sac that the Pharisees wanted to steer Jesus into. Instead, Jesus takes the conversation sideways and 'plays the same number'. In response to their question, he asks them about whether they knew who would be forgiven more – the person who owed the money-lender 500 denarii, or the person who owed the money-lender 50 denarii (Luke 7.41). Jesus both answers the question and mutates the answer for the benefit of those who think like a grasshopper.

The way that Jesus would take a question and look at it sideways on is also illustrated in the parable of the Good Samaritan. As it stands, it seems that the parable is given in response to a question that it does not appear to answer. Jesus is asked by an expert in the law to qualify the commandment 'to love your neighbour as yourself'. 'Who then is my neighbour?' is the question asked of him (Luke 10.29). The parable is an illustration of how to be a good neighbour, and is a challenge to the expert in the law since it is the pariah figure of the Samaritan who turns out to be the good neighbour. However, the parable does not attempt to answer the question of who might be considered as a neighbour.

Imagine a conversation as an ornate Italian square criss-crossed by four roads coming in and out. You can either go straight out of the square, continuing in the same direction you were travelling when you came in, or you can turn to the left or to the right and go out of the square at right angles to the way you came in. Much of the time when Jesus talks in public, he takes the words spoken by the other person and then sends them off in another direction. When he was told that his family were standing outside waiting to see him (Luke 8.19–21), Jesus used the idea of family to reflect on the nature of commitment and belief: 'My mother and brothers are those who hear God's word and put it into practice.' If this is read as the equivalent of Jesus going into the square and straight out in the same direction, in other words as a logical progression of thought, then it can come across as quite harsh. It appears to suggest that Mary and his brothers are not important to Jesus, or at least no more important than anyone else who does the will of God. From this angle, Jesus can seen quite detached. The same impression can be gathered from the incident at the wedding feast, when Jesus says to his mother that her concern is not his concern because his hour is not yet come (John 2.4). However, if these exchanges are read as the equivalent to Jesus heading into and then turning left or right out of the square – in other words as a lateral train of thought pivoting on what the other person has said – then they can be more properly understood as Jesus intentionally taking the conversation off in another direction. Mary and the Syro-Phoenician woman both question Jesus on an immediate, temporal level, but they recognize the twist that Jesus gives to the conversation and respond to him on the deeper spiritual level that is triggered by his comment.

Caterpillar and Grasshopper Interaction

Jesus is perfectly capable of a straight caterpillar-type answer, but these more unequivocal statements tend to be made when he is alone with his disciples and there is something that needs explaining. When Peter asks how many times he should forgive another, Jesus answers, 'not seven times, but seventy-seven times' (Matthew 18.22). 'Caterpillar conversations' occur when people understand what he is saying and Jesus is either commenting or explaining further. For example, when the centurion talks about how he perceives Jesus' power, Jesus exclaims in reply that he has never seen such faith anywhere in Israel (Luke 7.9).

The interaction of these two types of conversational approach is demonstrated most clearly after the transfiguration when Jesus appears to Peter, James and John with Moses and Elijah. After this revelation, Jesus tries to explain in a straightforward, logical manner what is shortly going to happen: he will need to travel from Galilee to Jerusalem where he will be killed, and after three days will rise again from the dead. This is a step-by-step, caterpillar-like explanation. It is given in the context of three of the disciples having just seen him with Moses and Elijah so there is a chance they might be able to understand the underlying reality of what is going on.

In fact, the disciples do not have a clue what he is talking about (Mark 9.32). Jesus was a successful, small-town preacher in Galilee; he pulled big crowds and performed miracles. The idea of him needing to go to the big city where he would end up getting killed makes no sense at all to them. Because the disciples do not understand what he is saying, Jesus has to move from caterpillar-type explanation to grasshopper-type illustration. Thus, in the next conversation recorded between Jesus and his disciples, he does not follow the line of thought they introduce. They want to know about who will be the greatest in the kingdom of heaven; he takes the illustration of a child to challenge them on what they meant by being the greatest. He is mixing some previously unrelated concepts – kingdom and service – so he jumps in and out of ideas, as if to say, 'Here's another way of looking at it'.

Both grasshopper and caterpillar approaches are important at different times for different purposes. The prophet in the Old

Testament was a classic grasshopper figure. The task of the prophets was to look beyond the immediate and evidential. They did not so much predict the future as make people aware of the consequences of their behaviour. This often involved the grasshopper's intuitive leaps of imagination needed to push an idea forward. The prophets in the Old Testament were called by God to 'remind' Israel of the expectations of the covenant. The etymology of 'prophet' is from the Greek, meaning 'one who speaks for someone else'. The Hebrew word for 'prophet' is from a root meaning 'to bubble forth, as from a fountain' (e.g. Psalm 45.1). Thus, a prophet is a person inspired to interpret the will of God.

The pastor has the classic caterpillar role. With the caterpillar approach there is the time, energy and precision to think through the details of what is being discussed. The task of the pastor is to nurture and care for the people committed to his care. 'Pastor' – from the Latin word for 'shepherd' – is often used to refer to the ordained minister who is charged with the primary spiritual care of a local church. The pastor has a special ability to effectively guide, feed and protect a flock of followers in Christ, a function also known as 'shepherding' (Ephesians 4.11).

The grasshopper approach can be over-used if the assumption is that people will necessarily have the knowledge and background information to understand the gospel message. However, if the caterpillar approach is over-used, and there is too tight a concern for everything to be explained and put into context, then the gospel can be deprived of a capacity to surprise.

A faith-based approach to life does not, by definition, conform to the patterns of this world (Romans 12.2) and therefore, to the outsider there can be something startling about a grasshopper-action or comment. When someone is surprised they look at something differently. On one occasion I was in a hurry to get a train back from London to Cambridge. It was 7.15 a.m. and I needed to be back in college at 9 a.m. to give a lecture. Walking towards the platform, I was asked for a cup of tea. I was busy, I was walking quickly and I did not stop. However, as I got on the train I thought that a cup of tea was a fair thing for someone to ask for at 7.15 a.m. I went back, found the person, missed my train but had the cup of tea with him.

7

Identity

———◦◦◦◦———

This chapter looks at the balance between how the faith might be presented and how the faith might be understood. If as 'an ambiguous evangelist' I am too persuasive and creative in presenting reasons for the faith then I run the risk of choice, rather than truth, becoming the justification for my belief. If this happens and choice, not truth, becomes the reason for belief, then the eventual result is one of two things – either sentimentality (it feels right to me) or else legalism (this is what I need to do).

The task of presenting the Christian faith is called 'apologetics'. Apologetics is derived from the Greek *apologia*, which means 'to create a defence', and is literally the attempt to make a defence for the Christian faith. It is answering the questions that people ask. Apologetics is the branch of Christian theology which has as its aim the reasoned advocacy of the Christian faith. It includes both positive arguments for the truth of Christianity and rebuttals of criticisms levelled at it. It is commended in Scripture:

> Always have the answer ready for people who ask you the reason for the hope that you all have. (1 Peter 3.15 Jerusalem Bible)

Answering the Questions Asked

Football is the classic way of illustrating the idea of a user-friendly, bite-size, formula presentation of Christianity. If someone thinks that football is a ridiculous sport then I am not going to arouse their interest by telling them the purpose of football is to score a goal. The more I talk about how the winger dribbles the ball down the touchline and then crosses it into the centre then the more ridiculous the game will appear. The role of an apologist is to translate football into terms that will appeal to the person listening. Thus, the apologist may talk about how football can provide a wider friendship base or about how playing football means that you will be physically fit and being physically fit would improve quality of life. These are benefits of the game that might appeal to anyone regardless of their interest or not in 11 men trying to kick a ball into the opponent's goal.

Translating this into evangelistic terms, forgiveness can be explained in terms of psychological well-being and how much better someone might feel if they do not hold onto a grudge against another person. Sexual chastity (1 Corinthians 6.18) can be discussed in terms of mental and emotional health and well-being. I will talk about the fact that there is good evidence that prayer is a natural instinct rather than a learnt activity. The RAC Foundation spoke to 898 motorists around the country during June 2003 as part of on-going research into commuting, and found that nearly 75 per cent of drivers admitted to saying the odd prayer when behind the wheel, while 22 per cent said that they prayed on a regular basis. People admitted to praying that the speed camera had no film, for lighter traffic and for no delays on their journey. However, people also prayed for others who were suffering, for families, friends and loved ones.

The apologist is asking the question 'Why not be a non-Christian?' rather than 'Why be a Christian?' Any apologetic Christian teaching will be correlated to the questions which the secular culture is asking of the young person. Tillich (1951) wrote that the fatal pedagogical error is to throw answers like stones at the heads of those who have not yet asked the questions. There is something deeply unappetizing about hard, granite-like slabs of Christian truth being thrown at people who are either unaware or uninterested. A friend, while helping as a volunteer at Crisis at Christmas, was taken to be someone homeless by one of the other volunteers. With a minimum introduction he was asked whether he knew Jesus Christ as his Lord and Saviour. My friend was deeply frustrated at this clumsy approach and his angry retort was, 'Yes, I do; now please get lost!'

In the interest of making my faith relevant, authentic and real to a non-believer, I will happily use every image, idea or cultural echo available to trigger their thoughts and imagination. Dido, for example, sang about how a thoughtful lover gave her a towel as she came in from the rain, which transformed a terrible day into the best day of her life. This song gives a bridging illustration of the day-to-day reality of Christ's incarnation. In this way, I can quite literally learn my theology through popular art and culture.

Finding an Adequate Paradigm: Understanding God

There is a danger that a way of presenting the faith becomes a way of understanding the faith. When this slippage occurs, the very correct task of presenting the faith in ways that people can understand and interpret within their own framework becomes synonymous with how faith is understood. There is a thin dividing line between 'contextualization' and 'depends on the situation'; between 'relevant' and 'relative'; between 'personal' and 'a matter of opinion'. There is a distinction, though, that needs to be drawn between a response to the truth and a perception of the truth.

The idea that perception of truth is as important as truth itself can be categorized as 'post-modern'. 'Post-modern' is a contested term taken to refer to a variety of contemporary features, including a diminishment of the power and efficacy of society's structures, and a consequential rise in the significance given to the individual's thoughts, feelings and decisions. Lyotard (1984) talked about an incredulity towards all meta-narratives. Harvey (1992) wrote about how the cultural pathology of modernism was alienation and the cultural pathology of post-modernism was fragmentation.

> We can no longer conceive of the individual as alienated in the classical Marxist sense, because to be alienated presupposes a coherent rather than a fragmented sense of self from which to be alienated. (Harvey, 1992:53)

Taylor (1992) said that the price of individualism is a loss of purpose because we no longer have a bigger picture of events. Everything is judged simply on the basis of how it affects me. If all that exists consists of interpretations, then the idea of truth as a simple correspondence to a set of affairs that actually happened – the facts of the matter – falls victim. In contrast, God is still God, however someone might choose to respond to him.

I, as an apologist, will want to present the story of the crucifixion in a way that will help people listening to understand it and to engage with its significance. However, the point of the cross being a 'stumbling-block to Jews and foolishness to Gentiles' (1 Corinthians 1.23) is that it is startling and cannot be easily understood, and if it can't be easily understood, it can't be easily explained. If I am constantly making my presentation reaction-dependent, then the danger is that in my desire to connect with people's situation I might have inadvertently undercut the challenge of the gospel message.

Theology needs to underpin anthropology. The fatherhood of God is not based on a human understanding of fathers, but rather is the primary source of all fatherhood (Ephesians 3.15). Someone is wise because they fear God (Proverbs 1.7); they don't fear God because they are wise. All life is an act of worship (Romans 12.1) but worship is something more than just day-to-day living. 'God is love' (1 John 4.16) is theology; 'love is God' is emotivism. Unless self is properly recognized as being understood through understanding God (rather than vice versa) then what is left is a pathological (either emotion- or duty-based) understanding of the gospel in which reaction and what is felt or done in response becomes all-important.

One of the findings of our youth and world view research was that the interviewees were self-defining themselves as being happy. They were not living their lives with a developed sense of angst, inadequacy and lack of fulfilment. Generally, the young people we talked with were enjoying the lives on offer to them through an immersion in popular art and culture. I have found that when I present these findings to church groups and conferences, there has been a uniform uneasiness at the idea of people considering themselves to be happy – 'How can they know?', 'Are they sure?' 'They will find out!' were typical of the different reactions. It seemed as if the idea of happiness was a challenge to the paradigm of the Church's engagement: if people were happy, how then could they be made to realize their need of forgiveness in Christ?

This raises the question of why the Church seems to expect, or even need, such a realization. I would argue that a presentation of the cross on the basis that someone should realize their need of forgiveness is an inadequate paradigm for mission. There are deep flaws within a pathological presentation of Christianity where the validity of the message is wholly dependent on the hearer realizing their need of salvation. There is a sermon, which occurs repeatedly in different versions, that concentrates on Jesus dying on the cross; the challenge of this sermon is for the listener to realize how much Jesus loves them and to respond in kind. Such a slant on the crucifixion always leaves me feeling exposed. My feeling when I hear such a message is that I can't compete, and to try to compete would be responding out of guilt rather than joy. If someone is put into a position where their response to the Christian message comes more out of need than choice then they will demonstrate their Christian faith as obligation rather than as grace. My primary response to the cross is worship. My secondary response to the cross is obedience. My obedience is an expression of my worship.

The need for God to be relevant comes after the need for God to be understood. I have to understand God before I know how to respond to God. In Christ the Priest, there is a mediatorial and reconciling nature (Hebrews 4.14). This peace-making role is commended in the Beatitudes (Matthew 5.9). The Son of Man came not to be served but to serve and to give his lifer as a ransom for many (Mark 10.45). This same approach is asked of the Christian. In all these instances it is God who comes first and me who comes second. Understanding God then helps me to understand myself. It is the theology that defines the anthropology; the true nature of personhood is realized through understanding the true nature of God.

This understanding of the nature of God provides a template both of how to understand oneself and also how to behave with other people. For example, with an understanding of God's grace, I can grasp hold of the idea that I am not predetermined to continually make the same mistakes. The fact that someone has treated me badly does not mean that I am automatically going to do the same thing to someone else. If a core idea of grace is a recurring present-ness of the reality of God's love and acceptance, and if I can base my actions on this underpinning reality, then I am in a better position to make clear decisions dictated primarily by a desire to bring glory to God. Or, to take another example, if someone has an adversarial approach to life, assuming themselves to be in competition with everyone else, then the incarnation of Christ, his taking human form and coming among people as a servant, provides a model for empathetic involvement in other people's lives.

Identity as a Route to Understanding

Identity in Christ is the heart of the salvation message, and identity and personal story are key contemporary themes. This is illustrated in *Finding Nemo*: a film animation featuring Nemo, a young clownfish. When Nemo is stolen from his coral-reef home, his timid father searches the ocean to find him. Nemo's father has different adventures but one single identity and purpose in the film – which is to find his son. One of the ideas associated with post-modernism is that an individual has multiple identities.

> Everything is possible but nothing connects . . . Go for something that makes sense by making nonsense . . . Who is real? Who is a replicant? Who cares? Enjoy. (Polhemus, 1998: 132–133)

I have multiple ways of relating to the world (parent, lover, child, clubber, sportsman, friend, etc.) but in Christ I have a single identity as a created child of God. The Christian message of salvation is classically described as being 'loved by God'. I prefer the idea of being known by God, and the idea of salvation as being known by God is the ultimate antidote to any connection between ideas of ambiguity and uncertainty. 'Now we see but a poor reflection as in a mirror; then we shall see face to face. Now I know in part; then I shall know fully, even as I am fully known' (1 Corinthians 13.12).

For much of his life, Proust was sickly. The appeal of Proust, suggests Alain de Botton (1997), is his endless interest and fascination in and knowledge of the details of his friends' lives, largely as the result of his being a bedridden hypochondriac. When his friends came to visit, he would listen to their stories and would tell them, '*N'allez pas trop vite*' (Don't go so quickly), because the significance would always lie in the detail of their lives.

People need to feel known in order to feel that they belong. When my father died and when a long-term relationship finished, I had a particular feeling or sensation that was the same in each case. It was the loss of my story: people who knew me in a way that no others did had gone. When in *EastEnders* Dot Cotton retired from her job in the launderette, she talked with Pauline and asked what she had achieved. Pauline's reply was that Dot should remember all the people who had come into the launderette, drunk a cup of coffee and talked with Dot about what was going on in their lives. In other words, the significance of Dot's life was in all the people she had known and who had known her. The popularity of reality TV is the fascination of knowing what the contestants are doing throughout the programme. The popularity of *I'm a Celebrity, Get Me Out of Here* and *Big Brother* are examples. The draw for the contestants is that people will know them. There is a type of fame in our society that is famous just for being famous; known just because you are known.

God knows what we want before we even ask it of him (Matthew 6.8). A sense of self is realized through each individual person being deeply and totally known by God.

I am convinced that neither death nor life, neither angels nor demons, neither the present nor the future, nor any powers, neither height nor depth, nor anything else in all creation, will be able to separate us from the love of God that is in Christ Jesus our Lord. (Romans 8.38–9)

8

Sculpting the Self

Sara Savage

def. Christian: like Christ, little Christ

Evangelism is in the business of helping people to know and become *like Christ*. How one person becomes like another person is in part sculpted by how we think *about persons*. This kind of thinking is often unspoken, so in this chapter I aim to make explicit various *models of person* implicit in Christian thinking today. How we think about persons will influence how we do evangelism, and what the short- and long-term effects of our evangelism are likely to be.

I will suggest three models that I believe are embedded in various strands of Christian discourse: a container model of person, a relational model of person and a narrative model of person.

Each of these models sculpts the self in different ways. Some facets of personhood, and relationship between an individual and God, are constructed, while others are shaved away. There is a two-way traffic: our understanding of God prompted by these models sculpts the self, and the way we sculpt self will also influence our Christian experience.

The three models I will discuss are 'true' insofar as any model can accurately represent a reality that extends far beyond the limits of our human knowing. We will see that while each model is consistent with Scripture, each model has its limitations and bias. No one model can tell the whole story of how God and human persons inter-relate.

The Container Model of Person

The early Greek philosophers were much exercised about 'substance'. Of what kind of 'stuff' is the universe made? In an age well before physics and cosmology, this was an important question, and a subject of much debate. Is the universe made of only one 'stuff' (monism) or two (dualism)?

Dualism argues that the material stuff of the universe is different from the spiritual stuff. Further, the material stuff gets a negative press: matter decays, corrupts, is transient and, in some quarters, was thought to be inherently evil. This spiritual stuff could be thought of in a variety of ways, such as gods, spirits, pure thought, or eternal 'ideals' such as geometric forms.

The human person clearly has some material attributes, most notably the human body, visible to all in its various states of growth and decline. But the human person is more than that. At the very least, the human person can think lofty thoughts, and can imagine, for example, pure mathematics. This side of the human person is more akin to the untarnished spiritual stuff of the universe.

Thinking about the human person as a material container housing spiritual stuff made sense in the ancient Greek world. Some people thought of *all* human persons possessing an eternal spirit, because spiritual stuff is, *by definition*, eternal. (Note that this is not a biblical idea!) Thus, the container model of person has a long, somewhat independent, history apart from Hebrew ways of thinking found in the Old Testament. It was only later that this Greek way of thinking seeped into the cultural mishmash that Israel, after the exile and under Roman occupation, had become. This doesn't mean that the container model is wrong, but neither can we claim it is of purely biblical origin.

How then does this model of person influence our thinking

and evangelism today? I will draw upon common figures of speech and phrases from worship songs which hint at the presence of this model. I will then suggest ways in which this model of person shapes our Christian experience, our understanding of ourselves and of God.

> Do you have Christ in your life?
> Have you been filled with the Holy Spirit?
> Have you received grace/forgiveness/eternal life?
> Receive the Word of the Lord!
> I pour out my heart to You
> She received her first communion.
> Receive your healing, in the name of Jesus!
> I cast out this demon in the name of Jesus!

The hints can also be seen in lines from contemporary worship songs:

> Come down O love divine, fill thou this soul of mine
> (Bianca da Siena)

> Breathe on me breath of God, fill me with life anew.
> (Hatch)

> Jesus put this song into our hearts
> (Kendrick)

> In faith, receive from him
> (Evans)

> Freely, freely, you have received
> (Owens)

> More love, more power, more of you in my life
> (de Hiero)

Your holy presence living in me
(Burnett)

In the above examples, the whole point of the container is what it contains. It is the 'spiritual stuff' poured in that gets the air time. The earthly container is appropriately humbled through neglect. The solution for a human person understood as a container crammed with bad, sinful things is to empty it, and then re-fill the container with good, spiritual things. Christ (fully human) is also understood as a container; yet Christ is an entirely 'Good Container' who receives into himself little Christian containers:

Let me ever more abide hidden in thy wounded side
(17th century, tr.)

Let me hide myself in thee
(Toplady)

Let me to thy bosom fly
(C. Wesley)

Take me deeper into You
(Dave Bryant)

Container thinking draws on ample biblical material. The scriptural injunction to 'Abide in me, and I in you' is clearly evidenced in both sections of the above stanzas and figures of speech. Interestingly, while searching through hymn and song books, I did observe that references to Christ as the 'Good Container' (suggesting a world-shunning piety) are found more frequently in older hymns. This contrasts with the greater emphasis in contemporary worship on filling the human person/container located *in* this world. Models can go through phases, too!

A more hygienic variation on Christ as the Good Container is the Church as a Collective Container. The Church, for some, can be understood as a container holding a collection of private, separate individuals. When the primary vehicle for relationship with God is carried by the Collective Container, then getting the social structure right is vital, as this is what gives shape to the container. It follows then that the symbolic, ritual representations of that social structure must also be correctly performed. There is little attempt to reveal the persons within the container, because, frankly, that is none of your business. As long the shape of the Collective Container is properly maintained, nothing more needs to be done. This broad brush cartoon of the church as an institution is sketched here to illustrate a point. What adherents to the Church as a Collective Container so often abhor about a Christianity based on the more personal container model of person is simply the *invasion of privacy*.

Leaving the more traditional forms of the model behind, and returning to the container model of person first discussed, what are its advantages for our understanding of ourselves and God, and thus for evangelism?

First, the container model has the virtue of simplicity. If you have only 20 minutes in which to explain the complex dynamics of salvation to the 'unsaved', you will probably draw on this model. 'Do you have Christ in your life?' What else provides this kind of shorthand?

Second, in an age where commercial transactions define many human relationships, the container model makes sense. Christ pours his divine life into us; we pour out our gratitude, or sin, or prayer requests, in response. Social exchange theory is supported by robust evidence that we tend to understand *relationship* in terms of balancing what we give against what we receive. As human beings we are rationally motivated to get at least as much as we give. Thus the container model ensures its own survival by motivating acceptance of the gospel: what a bargain! It would be illogical to refuse!

The container model of person makes human–divine transactions very easy. One simply has to offer up some things (sin, unbelief, wrong desires) and receive into the container

131

(salvation, eternal life, Jesus, etc.) And it's quick. In an age of fast food and Broadband, the speed of this transaction is important. If we were to pay for some item which took six months to be delivered, we would suspect that item doesn't really exist. Is it all a scam?

Vitally, all these factors – the simplicity, ease, generosity and rapidity afforded by the container model – all speak loud and clear of God's grace. The model works! God is found by those who seek him.

What then are the limitations of the model? The model implies that the container is inert. Certain kinds of passivity are likely to result. While the older hymns place more emphasis on abiding in Christ (he is the Good Container) or residing (more impersonally) within the Collective Container, the resultant withdrawing from the world suggests inactivity. Many modern worship songs focus on own containers being filled. I am not the first to point out the passive self-centredness of some aspects of contemporary worship. The cult of the self has become the building-block of contemporary Western culture and, in this regard, the container model again makes sense, as long as the emphasis is on our container being filled at Christ's expense (rather than Jesus' container being filled at our expense).

The container model implies hierarchy. The spiritual stuff is clearly much better than the material stuff. This is further echoed in Cartesian body/mind dualism. The mind, and thus all those who have access to the things of the mind, has much greater value. The elevated status of white, middle-class, well-educated, cerebral males within the Church (and in society as a whole) is well documented. Traditionally, churches have been organized as hierarchies, and hierarchies are bound to elicit certain behaviours between persons of vastly unequal power: fear, passivity, dependence, envy, gossip (the currency of the disempowered) on the one hand, and superiority (which can take the guise of *noblesse oblige*), control, and at the extreme end, religious abuse. This is not to blame the container model for all the ills of church history, but rather to point out the concordance between the container model and hierarchical human organizations.

Is plummeting church attendance within many traditional churches in the industrialized West also a sign of the demise of this model of person? Or is the container model of person still very much alive? Probably the latter. The Church now languishes amidst an unfair array of exciting secular 'fillers' such as football and shopping malls open 24/7. (It must be admitted that alternative spiritualities have been exaggerated as a significant threat to Christendom; people would simply rather go shopping.) And so we have fillers and more fillers.

Perhaps this competition over rival fillers adds to Christian suspicion concerning what kind of substances should fill the containers. Contemporary Christian discourse recycles Christian 'branding' as a way of identifying which fillers are acceptable, and which are not. Incidentally, this is good commercially for the Christian world. In the USA, while it may not be acceptable for Christians to stuff themselves with the thrills of secular amusement parks, to visit a *Christian* amusement park is considered edifying. And so we need Christian T-shirts, Christian nutritional advice, and so on. While contemporary Christians are clearly having a lot more fun than container Christians of a previous age (when nearly all sensory input was suspect, save for the hearing of the Word), the issue about what kind of substance fills the container is still very much alive.

The container model also makes clear who shall be praised for belonging to the in-group, and who shall be derogated for belonging to the out-group. The boundaries are clear. 'Membership badges' for the in-group are today mostly displayed through a styled use of language: 'I have Christ in my life, do you?' How we use language in church circles really matters; there are few other on-the-spot 'breathalyser' tests for group membership. (Behaviour takes much longer to observe.) The rules of the discourse, or way of using language, dictate what can be spoken and what needs to remain unspoken. Our shared Christian life becomes a collective maintenance of a discourse; this is what outsiders and sociologists tend to observe (and not much else).

Perhaps the greatest disadvantage is the way the container model can engender magical thinking. Magical thinking underlies our pragmatically motivated attempts to gain specific outcomes through 'working' spiritual powers or incantations. 'I claim this answer to prayer in the name of Jesus' reveals some structural similarities to the waving of a magic wand. The passivity of the container leaves it little else it can do. By its very nature the container is disqualified; it is not 'good enough' to act. It would be unspiritual to do so. Saying or believing the right thing becomes crucial, in the hope that the desired result will 'happen by faith' (delivered – without a middleman – directly to the container).

Magical thinking shrinks the size of the believer's 'problem space'. A problem space, as in a chess game, consists of the array of all possible moves in response to a given challenge. If the problem space is circumscribed through ignorance, the player won't be able to find the best move. Christians loyal to the container model possess fewer possible 'moves' beyond waiting for God's answer to prayer, following the pronouncements of the right words or thoughts. While God certainly does answer prayer, as co-designers of our lives there remain many things which we have to do for ourselves, in concert *with* God. However, the container model does not allow for that. Thus the personal problems of many Christians remain unresolved, while people wait for the slow gait of God who is required to circumnavigate the closed world we have created by a model which is, as all models are, only partly true.

Inevitably, traditional forms of evangelism have drawn on the container model of person for its clarity and simplicity in order to make the gospel known within one short session. Through it people have been enabled to know Christ. Why complain? I complain because the disadvantages of the container model come into play later down the line. By it, not only is self-understanding limited, but also our understanding of God; God as Filler may revolve simply around his divine 'use-value'.

The Relational Model of Person

In 1902 the sociologist Cooley coined the term 'the looking-glass self' to convey how our sense of self is constructed through what is reflected back to us by significant others. Some decades later, psychologists within the British object relations school challenged Freud's biological reductionism and argued that it is relationship with *another* that people crave from their earliest moments and throughout their life. Africans have known this for a long time, as expressed in the African proverb: 'we are all persons because of other persons'. The potent image of the infant Christ gazing into the face of his mother has, throughout the ages, given shape to our longing for the loving gaze which confers a sense of self. In recent decades, theologians have also moved in a direction which emphasizes the social nature of God: God himself is a community of persons, and his purpose throughout the story of redemption is to draw people into a relationship with the divine community of Persons. This relational model of person is also clear in Scripture: 'May the Lord bless you . . . and make his face to shine upon you', says the Aaronic blessing. Many contemporary Christian songs and hymns reflect this understanding of both human and divine persons as relational beings:

> He looks down upon us, delight in his face
> (Kendrick)

> As we gaze on Your kingly brightness
> (Kendrick)

> Open our eyes Lord, we want to see Jesus
> (Cull)

The relational model of persons in contemporary worship has not simply eliminated the container model of person. Rather, both models can often be seen intermingling as worshippers 'reach out', 'receive', 'touch', 'gaze' and 'overflow'. The presence of the relational model has brought about significant shifts in Christian thinking. To establish mutuality between persons (however unequal) does mean that we cannot go on simply ignoring the container. And so evangelism has moved from the hit-and-run 'tent crusade' to the establishment of friendship evangelism over a period of time. We come to know Christ through knowing a 'little Christ' (Christian). And today, many Christians are hungering for ways in which they can harness the whole of their persons – body, mind, emotions and spirit – into a relationship with God. Worship leaders encourage us to lift hands, hearts, voices, indeed our entire beings, to God, enabling an integration of the previously separated container-spirit.

Through the relational model of person in Christian worship and teaching, people are encouraged better to understand themselves and other people. To love God unavoidably involves loving our neighbour *as ourselves*, and this includes an appropriate regard for the self. This regard needs to be distinguished from self-love or grandiosity, that fragile defence against a damaged sense of self which distorts relationship with others and with God.

As the developer of the Beta course, I have written so extensively about this elsewhere (Savage, Watts and Layzell, 2003; Savage in Begbie, 2000) that it seems unnecessary to repeat much of it here. The relational model of person for spiritual growth is enormously fruitful. For readers wondering what a relational model of persons looks like fully blown, please visit www.beta-course.org (The Beta Course: Being Christian – Becoming Whole – Building Community).

As fully committed to the relational model of person as I am, are there any shortcomings I can acknowledge? First, all good models can be short-circuited and end up as a caricature. The relational model of person could, badly managed, produce a body of Christians who are endlessly absorbed by their own feelings and needs, addicted to finding the perfect relationship that will make them whole. Combined with the container model, more good feelings and more 'experience' are endlessly needed to shore up a fragile sense of self. The desire for the blissful experience of community can decompose into a holy huddle, with serving the community far down the list of priorities. Churches need not go down this route (and many churches are now placing serving the community at the top of their agenda), but it takes skilled handling to manage the flood of pastoral need and longing for relatedness, once the floodgates are opened.

It is a risk worth taking. To dam up personal need out of a fear of self-absorption will confine people to a permanently crippled state. Denying their own woundedness, people remain of limited use to others. Part of the rationale of the Beta course is therefore to provide enough resources so that the flood of pastoral need can be at least partly met, and then steered towards service to others.

A more serious challenge to the relational model of person is personal suffering. What happens if God should choose to hide his face from the beloved? It happens. St John of the Cross calls it 'the dark night of the soul'. In such an experience, no amount of singing of worship songs will restore the sense of well-being based on the experience of being loved. Where can the believer go when: the dark night has descended, or catastrophic suffering hits (and it feels as if that Presence has disappeared), or incrementally it has become apparent that life won't turn out how you thought it should?

It may be that while a person remains centred around his/her own legitimate human need for well-being, the relational model of person may be insufficient to help deal with a disastrous loss of well-being based on being positively reflected in the mirror of another Person. Should this be the case, I suggest incorporating another model of person (into the mixture of container and relational models): the narrative model.

The Narrative Model of Person

A narrative model of person proposes that each one of us constructs our sense of self through a narrative or story about our own lives. Story is considered by many to be the most basic cognitive structure by which human beings organize meaning. Story organizes our experience of time itself. Without story connecting one event to another, we would experience time as a continuous flow of the present. Story answers a key question: what is going on here? Babies are born understanding the basic form of a story: beginning–middle–end. When playing cooing or babbling games with babies, if a game is interrupted before the mood of the game has gone through all three phases, babies demonstrate distress (Rowe, 1995).

In line with developments in cognitive psychology, the narrative model of person views the human person as an actively engaged meaning-maker. As humans we construct our own sense of self through the interpretations (meanings) we place on the events and realities around us. As the psychologist Dorothy Rowe declares: 'You are your meaning system. Your meaning system is you' (Rowe, 1995).

This constructivist paradigm in therapy and counselling is quite acerbic. It could be paraphrased as saying to the client: 'Take responsibility for the way you have organized your perception of life; you can change it.' The cognitive therapist has the job of helping clients to understand, step by step, the implicit foundations beneath their everyday thoughts and perceptions. Cognitive therapy, and indeed psychotherapy more generally, helps people to bring into conscious awareness the template through which they view life.

In constructing our own life story via the interpretations we place on our own experience, we imbibe some aspects from our cultural milieu, and some from our collective unconscious (which, according to Jung, is the repository of racially inherited cognitive structures called 'archetypes'). Basic stories such as fairy tales reveal archetypes. For example, in western culture, basic stories are often about the struggle to be good. Such stories end 'happily ever after' with the joy of reward. Stories such as the Herculean tasks, 'Jason and the golden fleece', or the fairy tales where the innocent girl is set impossible tasks by an evil witch, and then eventually rescued by the handsome prince, all share a basic pattern: the struggle to attain worthiness, and the eventual attainment of reward.

These stories ring true with human experience. They echo the kinds of experiences we are likely to have in childhood, concerning the dilemma of having to be 'good'. In childhood, most of us have to bury or hide much of our selves (our emotions, anger, spontaneity or sexuality). Over time, we come to view the parts we learn to hide as 'bad'. Children do this at great cost to themselves, yet they have to do this in order to be accepted by parents, teachers, society, the Church. This experience of suffering in the process of trying to be good, and then finally being rewarded, is a basic pattern in human experience.

In a similar vein, the array of moral philosophies has in common this dynamic tension between balancing the needs of the individual against the needs of the community. Differences between cultures reflect different ways of resolving this tension. Western culture favours the emergence of the individual, while many traditional cultures favour the maintenance of the group. In each culture, there is a conflict, and thus a story! Whatever our culture, the story of the struggle to be good, the sacrifices involved, and the hope for eventual reward 'make sense' of much of human existence.

In our research into how young people make sense of the world via the popular arts (Savage, Mayo and Collins, forthcoming), we discovered that many young people today make sense of life in terms of what we have called the happy midi-narrative. This narrative (story) proclaims: happiness is the purpose of life; there is no need to posit meaning elsewhere. Young people believe that, whatever befalls, happiness will prevail. While some bad things may happen in life, there are enough resources for young people (through family, friends and the

139

popular arts) to enable personal happiness to be attained. Many young people believe that life will turn out happy, because 'that's what life is for'.

What would happen then if we discover – alas! – that no matter how hard we try, we just can't manage to be good enough, or that life does not treat us fairly, and the hoped-for reward is not forthcoming? Our meaning system, our story, is devastated. Life no longer makes sense.

The Christian story, I would argue, is our most potent resource for re-organizing our meaning structure (in other words, our *selves*) when suffering hits, and life seems pointless and cruel. The story of Christ's life follows a basic story, but with a surprising twist. Jesus lived a generous, courageous, creative life in obedience to God. He was 'good' on all counts. But rather than being rewarded, he was crucified. He died and was buried. There was no 'happily ever after' in human terms. His enemies who crucified him did not suddenly see that they were wrong and that he was right. But those who belonged to Jesus, through his faithfulness (not theirs), came to understand that Jesus' resurrection was indeed God's vindication. The story resolves, but not in the expected way.

Propounding the necessity of story for theology, that Christian truth is not 'detachable' from story, a varied body of narrative theology has evolved. Sally McFague writes:

> [For] the Christian, the story of Jesus is *the story par excellence*. For in his story not only is the human struggle of moving toward belief, but in some way, that story is the unification of the mundane and the transcendent . . . [It shows us] God's way of always being with human beings as they are, as concrete, temporal beings who have a beginning and an end – who are, in other words, *themselves stories*. (1975:125, 139)

Christian teaching and worship songs have always celebrated the Christian story, so, in one sense, there is nothing new here.

Hymns throughout the ages have themselves taken a narrative form:

> O come O come Immanuel
> And ransom captive Israel
> Who mourns in lonely exile here
> Until the Son of God appears
> (18th century)

> O loving wisdom of our God!
> When all was sin and shame
> A second Adam to the fight
> And to the rescue came
> (Newman)

> 'Tis mystery all! the Immortal dies
> who can explore his strange design?
> In vain the first-born seraph tried
> to sound the depths of love divine
> 'Tis mercy all! let earth adore,
> let angel minds inquire no more
> (Wesley)

Christianity is indeed a narrative-based faith. To this we can add a narrative model of person, along with insights from cognitive psychology. We can become aware of our own meaning system, our own narrative, and intertwine this with Christ's narrative. We need to bring to light the meaning system ('template') through which we view life, as this governs how we respond to life. How do I make sense of life? Myself? Others? God? What kind of expectations do I have concerning how others are going to treat me? Through this kind of self-revealing exploration, our own personal narrative needs to be immersed into Christ's narrative, to be subverted by it, in order for transformation to occur. Thus an even greater intertwining of persons is possible: the intertwining of persons *as stories*.

The cognitive constructivist paradigm argues that a person's meaning system is synonymous with that person's self. We hold nothing more dear, nor fight more fiercely to protect, than our own meaning system. It is the organization of our *self*. Thus, to have our life story submerged into Christ's story is no less than a death of the old self and a resurrection – a re-organization of our meaning system along the lines of Christ's story.

This radical goal, which concerns how one person becomes like another Person, through the intermingling of stories, needs to be the ultimate aim of our evangelism. To this end we need to tell The Story, again and again. And we need to provide ways of enabling people to become aware of their own narrative, their own meaning system. Our youth and world view research (Savage, Mayo and Collins, forthcoming) demonstrates that story (as in films, TV soaps, and other narrative-based art forms) is precisely the kind of tool which enables people to face, at a safe distance, the pain and joy of their own life story. To this end, the Beta course uses insights from cognitive psychology and narrative-based arts to give people resources to connect with their own stories, and Christ's. And so I suggest that evangelism should seek to bring together the Christian Story and individual's own stories, via stories expressed in various art forms. Again, there is nothing new here; Jesus was a story-teller, through his parables, *par excellence*.

In extolling the virtue of story, I am not suggesting that the container model or the relational model is to be superseded by this more complex, and more demanding, narrative model of person. Rather each model complements the other. There is no need to dispense with the simpler models of person. What is required is to be open to enlarge our model of person by moving, whenever possible, in the direction of increasing complexity. The shortcomings of any one model become pernicious only if that model is adhered to the exclusion of all others. Ambiguity in evangelism, re-phrasing the title of this book, is not about having a vague message, but rather the confidence that no one model of person will suffice.

I would like to conclude by subverting my own ending! The

container model, in its simplicity, is often the first way we come to understand ourselves in relation to God. In developmental psychology, the principle of 'first in, last out' describes how the cognitive structures which are established earliest are generally the last to disappear, even under conditions of illness or dementia. Under great stress, regression to a simpler model of person may indeed be redemptive.

Imagine the final stage of Christ's passion. Jesus experienced being abandoned by God as he hung on the cross. To lose the loving gaze of the Father would have inflicted an immeasurable wound to his sense of self. The basic story he had learnt through his Jewish faith, that God vindicates the righteous, was torn apart through the vicious torture he was undergoing. How did Jesus manage to keep his sense of self from utter disintegration?

In his very last words we glimpse a return to the simple container model ensconced in the night-time prayer he learnt in childhood:

'Father, into your hands I commit my spirit'.

Note

Chapter 2

1. The term 'midi-narrative' was used in order to distinguish it from the idea of meta-narrative. Whereas a meta-narrative suggests a teleological influence – a universal truth that makes sense of life as an unfolding story on a grand scale (as in Marxism, Enlightenment 'progress' or Judaeo–Christian end times) – the world view of young people is on the more modest scale of life here and now, and is derived from the here and now, rather than from something beyond. However, it is not purely individualistic (mini), but communal. Hence, the prefix 'midi' is an attempt to indicate the scope of the story-line.

References

Publications

Allan, J. (1995) 'Popular religion', in Francis, L. J., Kay, W., Kerbey A. and Fogwill, O. (eds), *Fast-Moving Currents in Youth Culture*, Oxford: Lynx.

Aune, K. (2002) *Single Women: Challenge to the Church?*, Carlisle: Paternoster.

BBC *News* (2004) 'School "Daily Worship" Questioned', http://news.bbc.co.uk/go/pr/fr/-/1/hi/education/3646389.stm, 21 April, accessed 21 April 2004.

Beaudoin, T. (1998) *Virtual Faith: The Irreverent Spiritual Quest of Generation X*, San Francisco: Jossey-Bass Publishers.

Beaudoin, T. (2003) *Consuming Faith*, Oxford: Sheed & Ward.

Begbie, J. (ed.) (2000) *Beholding the Glory: Incarnation Through the Arts*, London: Darton, Longman & Todd.

Begbie, J. (2004) Personal conversation.

Bragg, M. (2003) *The Adventure of English*, London: Hodder & Stoughton.

Brierley, P. (1999) *UK Christian Handbook: Religious Trends*, London: HarperCollins.

Brierley, P. (2000) *The Tide is Running Out: What the English Church Attendance Survey Reveals*, London: Christian Research.

Brown, C. (2001) *The Death of Christian Britain*, London: Routledge.

Bruce, S. (1996) *Religion in the Modern World*, Oxford: Oxford University Press.

Bruce, S. (1999) *The Future of Liberal Christianity*, presentation made at the British Sociological Association Sociology of Religion Conference held at Exeter University.

Bruce, S. (2002) *God is Dead: Secularization in the West*, Oxford: Blackwell Publishing.

Cameron, H. (2002) 'The Community Involvement of Church Attenders: Findings of the English 2001 Church Life Profile', paper given at the ISTR Fifth International Conference, Cape Town, South Africa, July.

Church of England Mission and Public Affairs Council (2004) *Mission-shaped Church*, London: Church House Publishing.

Collins, C. (1994) *The Vision of the Fool*, Ipswich: Golgonooza Press.

Collins, S. (1997) *Young People's Faith in Late Modernity*, unpublished PhD thesis, Guildford: University of Surrey.

Cooley, C. H. (1902, 1964) *Human Nature and the Social Order*, New York: Schoken Books.

Cottrell, M. (1985) *Secular Beliefs in Contemporary Society*, unpublished DPhil thesis, Oxford: Oxford University.

Cox, E. and Cairns, J. M. (1989) *Reforming Religious Education: The Religious Clauses of the 1988 Education Reform Act*, London: Kogan Page.

Cox, M. (ed.) (1992) *Shakespeare Comes to Broadmoor*, London: Jessica Kingsley Publishers.

Davie, G. (2000) *Religion in Modern Europe: A Memory Mutates*, Oxford: Oxford University Press.

De Bono, E. (1973) *Lateral Thinking: Creativity Step by Step*, New York: Harper & Row.

De Botton, A. (1997) *How Proust Can Change Your Life*, London: Picador.

De Saint-Exupéry, A. (2002) *The Little Prince*, London: Egmont.

Dick, K. (1960) *Pierrot*, London: Hutchinson.

Dostoevsky, F. (1958) *The Brothers Karamazov*, London: Penguin.

Drane, J. (2000) *Cultural Change and Biblical Faith*, Carlisle: Paternoster Press.

Dykstra, C. (1981) *Vision and Character*, New York: Paulist Press.

Fernando, A. (2001) *Sharing the Truth in Love: How to Relate to People of Other Faiths*, Grand Rapids, MI: Discovery House Publishers.

Forster, E. M. (1924) *A Passage to India*, London: Arnold.

Francis, L. J. (2001) *The Values Debate: A Voice from the Pupils*, London: Woburn Press.

Fung, R. (2002) *The Isaiah Vision*, Geneva: WCC Publications.

Gill, R. (1999) *Churchgoing and Christian Ethics*, Cambridge: Cambridge University Press.

Gray, J. (2002) *Men are from Mars, Women are from Venus: How to Get What You Want in Your Relationships*, New York: HarperCollins.

Harvey, D. (1992) *The Condition of Post-modernity*, Oxford: Blackwell.

Heelas, P., Woodhead, L., Seel, B., Szerszynski, B. and Tusting, K. (2004) *The Spiritual Revolution: Why Religion is Giving Way to Spirituality*, Oxford: Blackwell.

Hervieu-Léger, D. (2000) *Religion as a Chain of Memory*, Cambridge: Polity Press.

Hornsby-Smith, M.P. (1991) *Roman Catholic Beliefs in England: Customary Catholicism and Transformations of Religious Authority*, Cambridge: Cambridge University Press.

Hull, J. (1999) *Religion in a Pluralist Society*, London: Routledge.

Hunt, S. (2003) 'The *Alpha* Programme: some tentative observations of state of the art evangelism in the UK', *Journal of Contemporary Religion*, Vol. 18, No. 1, pp. 77–93.

Jamieson, A. (2002) *A Churchless Faith*, London: SPCK.

Jeffers, S. (1997) *Feel the Fear and Do It Anyway: How to Turn Your Fear and Indecision into Confidence and Action*, New York: Rider.

Jowell, R., Curtice, J., Park, A., Thomson, K., Jarvis, L., Bromley, C. and Stratford, N. (2000) *British Social Attitudes: Focusing on Diversity*, London: Sage.

Lings, G. (2002) 'The Shape of Things to Come', presentation to the Church Army Chief Secretary's Conference, January and Joint Church Army Focus Group Conference, October. http://www.churcharmy.org.uk/sheffield_centre/copy_of_shape _things.htm, accessed 4 May 2004.

Lynch, G. (2002) *After Religion: 'Generation X' and the Search for Meaning*, London: Darton, Longman & Todd.

Lyotard, J. (ed.) (1984) *The Post-Modern Condition: A Report on Knowledge (Theory and History of Literature)*, Manchester: Manchester University Press.

McDonnell, J. (2003) 'Desperately seeking credibility: English Catholics, the news media and the Church', in Mitchell, J. and Marriage, S. (eds), *Mediating Religion: Conversations in Media, Religion and Culture*, London: Continuum, pp 33–43.

McFague, S. (1975) *Speaking in Parables*, Augsburg Fortress.

Macintyre, A. (1990) *After Virtue*, London: Duckworth.

Malbon, M. (1999) *Clubbing: Dancing, Ecstasy and Vitality*, London: Routledge.

Mayo, R. (1996) *Gospel Exploded*, London: SPCK.

Montefiore, H. (ed.) (1992) *The Gospel and Contemporary Culture*, London: Mowbray.

National Statistics Online (2003) 'Religion in Britain', http://www.statistics.gov.uk/CCI/nugget.asp?ID=293&Pos=6 &ColRank=1&Rank=176, published 13 February 2003, accessed 21 April 2004.

Newbigin, L. (1989), in *The Place of Christianity in Religious Education* (Action Group for the Encouragement of Religious Education).

Ofcom (2004) 'Review of Public Service Television Broadcasting', http://www.ofcom.org.uk/consultations/current/psb/sup_vol_ 1/audience/section1/?a=87101, published and accessed 21 April 2004.

Ostling, M. (2003) 'Harry Potter and the disenchantment of the world', *Journal of Contemporary Religion*, Vol. 18, No. 1, pp 3–23.

References

Polanyi, M. (1983) *Personal Knowledge*, London: Routledge & Kegan Paul.

Polhemus, T. (1998) 'In the supermarket of style', in S. Redhead (ed.), *The Club Cultures Reader: Readings in Popular Cultural Studies,* Oxford: Blackwell, pp. 130–133.

RAC Foundation (2003), London.

Richards, A. (2003) 'Interpreting contemporary spirituality', in Avis, P. (ed.), *Public Faith? The State of Religious Belief and Practice in Britain,* London: SPCK.

Richter, P. and Francis, L. J. (1998) *Gone But Not Forgotten: Church Leaving and Returning*, London: Darton, Longman & Todd.

Rowe, D. (1995) *Guide to Life,* London: HarperCollins.

Rowling, J. K. (1998) *Harry Potter and the Chamber of Secrets*, London: Bloomsbury.

Rylance, M. (1992) 'Hamlet and Romeo', in Cox, *Shakespeare Comes to Broadmoor*.

Savage, S. (2000) 'Through dance: fully human, fully alive', in J. Begbie (ed.), *Beholding the Glory: Incarnation through the Arts*, London: Darton, Longman & Todd.

Savage, S., Collins, S. and Mayo, B. (2003) *Theology Through the Arts for a New Generation: Empirical Research Report*, unpublished research report, Cambridge: Theology Through the Arts, Divinity Faculty, University of Cambridge and Centre for Youth Ministry, Ridley Hall Theological College.

Savage, S., Mayo, B. and Collins, S. (2005) *Explorations: The Worldview of Generation Y*, London: Church House Publishing.

Savage, S., Watts, F. and Layzell, R. (2003) *The Beta Course*, Cambridge: Cambridge University Press Printing Services.

Schwartz, B. (2004) *The Nature of Choice*, New York: Harper-Collins.

Sterk, H. (1993) 'Gender relations and narrative in a Reformed Church setting', in van Leeuwen, M.S. (ed.), *After Eden: Facing the Challenge of Gender Reconciliation*, Grand Rapids/Carlisle: Paternoster Press.

Taylor, C. (1992) *The Ethics of Authenticity*, Cambridge, MA: Harvard University Press.

Tillich, P. (1951) *Systematic Theology*, Chicago: University of Chicago Press.

Woodhead, L. (2004) *Spirituality Today: Findings from the Kendal Project*, paper presented at the British Sociological Association's Sociology of Religion Study Group Annual Conference, A Sociology of Spirituality, University of Bristol, 30 March 2004.

Wright, N. T. (1992) *The New Testament and the People of God*, London: SPCK.

Hymns and Songs

Bianca da Siena, B., tr. Littledale, R. F., from (1932) *The English Hymnal* no. 52, London and Oxford: A. R. Mowbray & Co. Ltd.

Bryant, D. (1978) 'Jesus take me as I am', © Thankyou Music, from (1991) *Songs of Fellowship* no. 443, Eastbourne: Kingsway Music.

Burnett, M. (1995) 'Breathe', from the album *Hungry*, Mercy/Vineyard Publishing ASCAP, Admin. by Vineyard Music Global Worldwide (1999) Vineyard Music UK.

Cull, R. (1976) © Maranatha Music/Word (UK) Ltd, from (1991) *Songs of Fellowship* no. 443, Eastbourne: Kingsway Music.

de Hiero, J. (1987) © Mercy Publishing/Thankyou Music, from (1991) *Songs of Fellowship* no. 392, Eastbourne: Kingsway Music.

Evans, D. J. (1986) 'Be still, for the presence of the Lord', © Thankyou Music, from (1991) *Songs of Fellowship* no. 40, Eastbourne: Kingsway Music.

Hatch, E., 'Breathe on me, Breath of God', from (1991) *Songs of Fellowship* no. 51, Eastbourne: Kingsway Music.

'Jesu, grant me this I pray' seventeenth century, tr. Sir H. W. Baker, from (1932) *The English Hymnal* no. 413, London and Oxford: A. R. Mowbray & Co. Ltd.

References

Kendrick, G. (1981) 'The King is among us', © Thankyou Music, from (1991) *Songs of Fellowship* no. 532, Eastbourne: Kingsway Music.

Kendrick, G. (1987) 'Shine Jesus shine', © Make Way Music, from (1991) *Songs of Fellowship* no. 362, Eastbourne: Kingsway Music.

Kendrick, G. (1988) © Thankyou Music, from (1991) *Songs of Fellowship* no. 299, Eastbourne: Kingsway Music.

Newman, J. H. 1801–90 'Praise to the Holiest in the height', from (1932) *The English Hymnal* no. 471, London and Oxford: A. R. Mowbray & Co. Ltd.

Owens, Carol (1972) 'God forgave my sin', © Lexicon Music Inc./U.N. Music Publishing Ltd, from (1991) *Songs of Fellowship* no. 129, Eastbourne: Kingsway Music.

Toplady, A. M. (1740–78) 'Rock of Ages, cleft for me', from (1932) *The English Hymnal* no. 477, London and Oxford: A. R. Mowbray & Co. Ltd.

'Veni veni Emmanuel', eighteenth century, tr. T. A. L., from (1932) *The English Hymnal* no. 8, London and Oxford: A. R. Mowbray & Co. Ltd.

Wesley, C. (1707–88) 'And can it be', from (1991) *Songs of Fellowship* no. 21, Eastbourne: Kingsway Music.

Wesley, C. (1707–88) 'Jesu lover of my soul', from (1932) *The English Hymnal* no. 414, London and Oxford: A. R. Mowbray & Co. Ltd.